Open Our Eyes
Seeing the Invisible People of Homelessness

Edited by Kevin D. Hendricks
Foreword by Chris Brogan

Published by Monkey Outta Nowhere
Saint Paul, Minnesota
www.MonkeyOuttaNowhere.com

Copyright © 2010 by Monkey Outta Nowhere
Design by Brian White
Layout by Ronald Cox

All rights reserved. No part of this book may be used or reproduced in any manner
whatsoever without permission, except in the case of brief quotations embodied in
critical articles or reviews.
ISBN: 1453721363
EAN-13: 9781453721360
Printed by CreateSpace in the United States of America

For Mark Horvath

" I am an invisible man. No, I am not a spook like those who haunted Edgar Allen Poe; nor am I one of your Hollywood-movie ectoplasms. I am a man of substance, of flesh and bone, fiber and liquids—and I might even be said to possess a mind. I am invisible, understand, simply because people refuse to see me. Like the bodiless heads you see sometimes in circus sideshows, it is as though I have been surrounded by mirrors of hard, distorted glass. When they approach me they see only my surroundings, themselves, or figments of their imagination—indeed, everything and anything except me. "

(the opening paragraph to *Invisible Man* by Ralph Ellison, 1952.)

Table of Contents

Foreword by Chris Brogan 9

Introduction by Kevin D. Hendricks 10

Steven: New Orleans 14

Sandra: Chicago 15

A Soul to Remember by Brad Abare 16

Angela: Atlanta 18

Five Things You Absolutely Must Know About Homelessness
by Shannon Moriarty 19

Mark: Detroit 22

Hero by Brandon Mendelson 23

Cecilia: San Luis Obispo, Calif. 24

Misconception #1: The Smelly, Dirty Homeless 25

Gypsy: Des Moines, Iowa 26

Compassion vs. Comparison by Jeff Lilley 27

Elvin: Batan Rouge, La. 29

Who is This Crazy Guy? by Heather Meeker 30

Coreen: Seattle 32

Drew: St Petersburg, Fla. 33

Misconception #2: It's Their Own Fault 34

James: Seattle 35

The Drive to Succeed by Scott Monty 36

Joni: New York 38

Social Media for Social Change by Natalie Profant Komuro 39

Jennifer: Los Angeles 41

Compassion Bridges Divides by Stephanie Rudat 42

Tom: Fayetteville, Ark. 44

We're All in This Together by Becky Kanis 45

Brianna: Wal-Mart Parking Lot in California 47

Misconception #3: Lazy 48

Eddie: Binghamton, N.Y. 49

Palliative Care for Those Living in Poverty? by Alan Graham 50

Jim: Las Vegas 52

Reflections on Homelessness by Jeff Holden 53

Mark: Phoenix 55

Misconception #4: Get a Job 56

Tony: Los Angeles 57

Nathan: Portland 58

Conversations and a Cup of Coffee by Michael Ian 59

Jody & Phillip: St. Paul, Minn. 61

A New Era in Problem Solving by Kari Saratovsky 62

David, Tish & Natasha: San Luis Obispo, Calif. 64

It Takes a Village by Lisa Truong 65

Jennifer: New York 66

Misconception #5: Panhandling for Substance Abuse 67

Marco & Cherese: Southern California 69

Hero by Example by Nedra Weinreich 70

Yong: Greensboro, N.C. 72

Ending Homelessness Requires Social Investors by David Henderson 73

Butch: Cleveland 75

Robert: Los Angeles 76

Social Media Matters by Wendy Cohen 77

Donald: New York 79

Misconception #6: Band Aids 80

Viper: Los Angeles 81

I Know Her Story by Jessica Gottlieb 82

Cotton: Greensboro, N.C. 83

Appreciative by Stefanie Michaels 84

Kathy: Austin, Texas 85

The Ecological Crisis Impacts Homelessness by Geoff Livingston 86

Steve: Los Angeles 88

Misconception #7: Let the Pros Do It 89

Karen: Detroit 90

Invisible People: Hardly Heard... Hardly Seen... Hardly Normal
by Lee Fox 91

Tracy: Austin, Texas 93

When is Enough Enough? by Chloe Noble 94

James: Detroit 96

God Loves Invisible People by Scott Williams 97

Jay: Cleveland 99

5 Practical Ways You Can Help the Homeless 100

A Word from Mark 103

Acknowledgements 105

Open Our Eyes: Seeing the Invisible People of Homelessness

Foreword

by Chris Brogan

If you asked him about me, Mark Horvath would tell you a story about shoes. He would make these reverent tones and reverent faces, and he'd say that he was touched that I gave him the shoes off my feet for him to give to a homeless person.

But that's silly. Because I'd only owned the shoes 10 minutes—they were a gift from Crocs. That gesture was more of a gesture than any salvation.

And yet, there's something in it, because the real leverage point of that is about Mark. Mark inspires me. Mark inspires hundreds and hundreds of people. I've never seen Mark take a stage and not finish the day without something more for the homeless to benefit from in the short term. Hanes gives him tons of socks. Ford gave him a car to drive across the country. Kodak gives him video cameras to shoot his films. We all give Mark money to push into service for the homeless.

See, that's just it. Mark isn't out there trying to fix the bigger issues, and sometimes that's a criticism he receives. Know what? Someone looking for a bite to eat or some warm socks can't wait for us to pass laws. They need it now. Mark is about the now.

How fitting, then, that I met Mark via Twitter, a service that's built on the now. Mark lives in that space between media and new media, in that space between talking about something and doing it passionately. He's the perfect reporter for the voiceless. He makes the invisible visible.

And for that, alone, you need to get into this book. It's going to move you, and it's going to inspire you, and if you don't *do something* when you're done, then it just means the problem is worse than we think.

I'm over here helping. How about you?

Chris Brogan is the *New York Times* bestselling author of *Social Media 101* and publisher of ChrisBrogan.com.

Web: ChrisBrogan.com
Twitter: @ChrisBrogan

Introduction

by Kevin D. Hendricks

A woman sits on the sidewalk with a cardboard sign, her hair stringy and her clothes disheveled. A backpack sits next to her with all her belongings. Her eyes are vacant and she watches as the people pass by, ignoring her.

Homelessness is easy to ignore. It's as simple as turning a blind eye and letting the homeless become invisible.

But not for Mark Horvath. Armed with a video camera and an iPhone, he walks up to that woman, looks her in the eye and talks to her. With her permission he starts up the camera and asks for her story. He snaps a photo with the iPhone and posts a link to Twitter, sharing her story with the world.

This is the work Mark Horvath does, making invisible people visible again.

In 2008 he launched the website InvisiblePeople.tv where he's posted more than a hundred stories of homeless people. Every one is unedited, raw and candid. The people come from all walks of life—drug addicts and pastors, grandmothers and pregnant moms, families and disabled veterans—and from all across the country—Los Angeles to New York, Florida to Seattle, New Orleans to Detroit, the forests of North Carolina to the snowy mountains of Alaska. Some have been homeless for as many as 40 years and some as few as 12 days.

"I thought nobody was telling their story, and I needed to go there," Mark told CNN in a 2009 report.

In 2009 Mark drove a loaner from Ford more than 11,000 miles across the country, meeting homeless people, passing out socks donated by Hanes and telling stories with the help of Twitter, Facebook and YouTube. "I was so worried driving in New York that I was going to wreck this car and Ford will never talk to me," Mark says. "It was one of the craziest things I've ever thought of and it happened."

In the spring of 2010 he traveled to Alaska with the help of Hertz to shine the light on homelessness in the North. In the summer of 2010 he hit the road again with another cross-country road trip.

Mark has been featured by the *L.A. Times*, CNN and NPR. He's spoken at a number of conferences and events, including SXSW, Blog World, GnomeDex and 140 Character Conference. The Huffington Post named him one of 11 Twitter activists you should follow. Pepsi awarded InvisiblePeople.tv a $50,000-grant as part of the user-voted SXSW Pepsi Challenge.

Mark captures the honest reality of homelessness at InvisiblePeople.tv. Each story is a reminder that anyone is a single crisis away from being homeless themselves. And so is Mark.

While Mark shares these stories he's on the edge of homelessness— for the second time in his life.

Far from a humanitarian rock star, Mark is formerly homeless himself. His life is a rollercoaster: He's been a drug dealer, a TV industry pro and a megachurch marketer. Mark has been around the block, and he's slept there, too.

His first business and marketing experience came as a 14-year-old drug dealer. In 1987 he bought a one-way ticket to California to make it in the music industry. The rock star plans didn't pan out, but he did find a successful career in the TV industry and by 1994 Mark proudly drove a Mercedes to work.

But it all came crashing down and Mark found himself homeless on the streets of Los Angeles. He survived by posing for tourist pictures with the help of a six-foot iguana, earning himself the title "Lizard Man of Hollywood Boulevard."

"It wasn't a career move," Mark says with typical understatement.

After a year on the streets Mark got back on his feet with the help of the Los Angeles Dream Center and climbed back to the top. In 2005 he had a six-figure income as a communications director in St. Louis. But then the economy tanked, Mark lost his job in 2007 and started that familiar spiral toward homelessness.

"The first time [I was homeless] I was on drugs and alcohol and did a lot of dumb things," Mark told NPR in a 2010 interview. "But this time I was doing everything right and I was still headed in that direction."

Open Our Eyes: Seeing the Invisible People of Homelessness

In the fall of 2008 Mark lived in a cockroach apartment in Los Angeles, freshly laid off from another job and facing foreclosure on his St. Louis home. "I lost a house before," Mark says on the Something Beautiful podcast, "But I was on heroin then—I liked it better the first time."

Being sober this time around meant understanding the reality of his own situation. This kind of insight helps Mark understand where homeless people are coming from—as he often remarks when people worry about the homeless and alcohol: "If you had to take a crap on the side of the street you'd want a drink too." Being sober doesn't make it easy.

"I was scared to death," Mark says. "I was going crazy. I needed something to do."

So in the fall of 2008, only seven weeks away from being homeless again, Mark started InvisiblePeople.tv.

Mark's situation hasn't changed since. He still lives in that cockroach apartment. He survives on donations, sponsorships and the occasional steady paycheck of a case manager position at a shelter in Glendale, Calif. The contents of his refrigerator include bottled water, some milk and a discounted vegetable tray.

All the while he tells the stories of the homeless, hoping not to become homeless himself.

"Don't waste a good crisis," Mark says. "Tonight there are people who were homeless that are sleeping inside because I had the courage—or I was dumb enough—to drive around the country."

Mark does it because he can't do anything else. He'd rather find a cushy job, a blonde and move to Hawaii, but he feels duty-bound to tell these stories, no matter what. He insists that he's not called to this work—he's forced into it.

"If you're called you can hang up the phone," Mark says. "I don't have any choice. I'm forced."

This book is inspired by Mark, dedicated to him and a tribute to his efforts. But it's not about him. "The story is people who are sleeping outside," says Mark. "It's not me."

In the following pages you'll find many of the stories Mark has gathered, retold in text. They're not nearly as raw and unedited as the videos on InvisiblePeople.tv, but they still tell the stories of the homeless and let them speak in their own words (they also include Mark's trademark question: If you had three wishes what would they be?). You'll also find reflections on homelessness, the power of social media and the incredible work Mark has accomplished—all from people who have been inspired by him. These voices include social media experts, nonprofit heroes, technology executives, a pastor and at least one formerly homeless person. Finally there are common misconceptions about homelessness and suggestions for ways you can get involved.

Mark often speaks of being 'wrecked' by the stories he's sharing. His comfortable world is turned upside down by the plight of others. The hope is this book will do the same to you. And that you'll be inspired to act.

Kevin D. Hendricks lives in St. Paul, Minn., with his wife, kids and two dogs. He runs his own freelance writing and editing company, Monkey Outta Nowhere. He's been blogging since 1998 and recently published *Addition by Adoption: Kids, Causes & 140 Characters*.

Web: KevinDHendricks.com
Twitter: @KevinHendricks

Supporting InvisiblePeople.tv
It's Mark's tenacious, inconvenient passion that has made this book possible. All profits from this book will go to support the work of the nonprofit organization InvisiblePeople.tv.

Steven

New Orleans

"We had a guy get 'bricked' the other night," says Steven, who has been homeless in New Orleans for six weeks. "Three guys just ran up and started throwing bricks at him. No reason, he was just sitting there doing nothing."

Without a door to lock, people like Steven are constantly vulnerable to violence. He worked all week and saved up $200, only to be robbed and lose his wallet, his ID and all his money. He plans to go back to work this week and try again.

"You know what I did before this? I was the minister, the resident pastor at the mission," Steven says, pointing across the street. He says they were doing things he didn't like and couldn't support, so he walked out. He's been homeless since.

Three Wishes:

1. Get the homeless a place to stay where they don't have to worry about anything.
2. The country would go down a different path and treat people better.
3. Bus ticket back to Colorado.

http://invisiblepeople.tv/blog/2009/08/steven-homeless-new-orleans-pastor/

Sandra

Chicago

Sandra lost her job, got evicted and what little she had was stolen, leaving her on the streets. This young woman panhandles to scrape together $40 to pay for a hotel each night, hoping to earn enough extra to afford a bus ticket home to Seattle.

Hundreds of people pass her as she sits on the west side of the Michigan Avenue Bridge, literally ignoring her. "Most people don't really pay that much attention," she admits. When asked about the safety and loneliness that can plague the homeless, she shrugs.

"As long as I got him, I'm OK," Sandra says, gesturing to the orange tabby cat in her arms. "It's hard. If it weren't for him I don't know what I'd do."

Three wishes:

1. Be able to go home.
2. A place to stay.
3. A job.

http://invisiblepeople.tv/blog/2010/01/sandra-homeles-chicago/

A Soul To Remember

by Brad Abare

"I have the shoes you gave her if you want them back," said our friend Dottie, in a trembling voice on the other end of the phone. My wife, Jamaica, began to tear up when she heard why the shoes were being returned.

A week earlier, we were in Pasadena, Calif., about 12 miles north of where Jamaica and I live in downtown Los Angeles. Although close to home, we were staying in a Pasadena hotel as I was participating in weeklong meetings that began early in the morning and went late into the evening.

On Monday and Tuesday nights during my week of meetings, Jamaica took the opportunity to hang out with a few of our homeless friends in the area, something we do together regularly.

On Monday night, our friend Medea was walking around barefoot after she had lost her shoes. In a blink, Jamaica took her own shoes off and gave them to Medea. When Jamaica came back to the hotel, she got out of the car and gave the keys to the valet (the only way to park at this hotel). The valet attendant noticed she was barefoot and asked if she was a guest at the hotel. "Yes, I'm in room 621." Jamaica then proceeded to walk through the fancy lobby and took the elevator up to our room. Barefoot!

The next night, we received the tear-filled call from Dottie. The call was to inform us of Medea's sudden death. Medea was found facedown in the dirt and was still wearing Jamaica's shoes that she had received the night before. From what we can gather, Medea died of liver failure.

For reasons different than the passing of those familiar to our lives, it's challenging to mourn the life of an invisible person. Who witnessed her life? Where is her family? Who will miss her? What impact did she have on people for the last half a century? Was Medea even her real name?

A week later, several of us gathered around the space Medea called home. Huddled behind a dumpster under the hum of power lines, we read Scripture and prayed amid the glow of a few candles. We shared memories of the Medea we knew so briefly and ended with a group recitation of the Lord's Prayer.

May each of us pursue the invisible people in our community so that Mark Horvath and his invisible people will be history, not headlines.

Brad Abare is the instigator behind ChurchMarketingSucks.com, founder of the Center for Church Communication, and a consultant with Foursquare and the Barna Group.

Web: BradAbare.com

Angela

Atlanta

Angela lives under a bridge. She coughs as Mark asks her what it's like living out here.

"Not good," she says, "But I'm surviving, I'm living."

How do you survive? "I believe in God," Angela says, nodding her head. She isn't sure how long she's been living under this bridge. She spends her days going to church and praying.

"Ya'll have a good day," she says with a nod and a smile.

Three Wishes:

1. "Good question, I'm not sure."

http://invisiblepeople.tv/blog/2009/09/angela-homeless-atlanta-gnomedex

Five Things You Absolutely Must Know About Homelessness

by Shannon Moriarty

Homelessness is a hot topic these days. It seems everywhere we look, the issue of homelessness is making a cameo. It's been all over the newspapers, on blogs, the 5 o'clock news—even on the cover of *Vogue*!

So while we have your ear, world, let us take advantage of this teachable moment. Here are five things about homelessness that you absolutely must understand in order to fully wrap your brain around this complex issue. Consider it a primer in reality.

Without further ado...

1. Homelessness is not a recession-induced phenomenon.

Remember the 1990s? The economy was booming, real estate was on the up and up, and it seemed everybody was profiting off of something. Well, not really.

Homelessness was an issue in the 1990s. In fact, homelessness has been a significant crisis in the United States since the 1980s. Although people will often cite the de-institutionalization of the mentally ill as the main impetus for the influx of homelessness in the 1980s, in reality, it was actually a combination of things. The 1980s is when the gap between the rich and the not-so-rich began to dramatically widen. The 1980s is when much of our nation's stock of affordable housing disappeared and housing discrimination based on race, gender and ethnic composition persisted. So while chronically homeless people may have been more noticeable on our streets, income inequality and persistent poverty have been major—and silent—causes of homelessness since the Reagan years.

2. To end homelessness, we need more affordable housing.

Today, there is no county in America where a person earning minimum wage can afford the median cost of housing. This lack of affordable housing stock means people who already have trouble making ends meet must use a larger portion of their income to pay for housing. Until the creation of decent, affordable housing becomes a priority at the federal and community levels, it is likely that more households will be "house poor" and thus vulnerable to falling into homelessness.

Open Our Eyes: Seeing the Invisible People of Homelessness

3. We need both sandwiches *and* solutions.

Amid the global recession, more and more people are in need of food, shelter and assistance. We cannot allow the basic needs of people in need to go unmet. Efforts to provide shelter beds, warm meals, clothing, short-term rental assistance and other "band-aid" solutions are critical for those who are struggling to survive.

So yes, pat yourself on the back for serving a meal in a soup line or participating in a donation drive.

But remember: Sandwiches alone will not solve anything. If you regularly participate in street outreach or volunteer at a homeless shelter, consider taking your involvement a step further by becoming involved in advocacy efforts. In order to truly combat the root causes of homelessness, we must address our lack of affordable housing, achieve healthcare reform, implement family-friendly workplace policies and take steps to eliminate poverty in America. We will not achieve the system-wide changes necessary to end homelessness by continuing to focus on band-aid solutions, necessary though they may be.

4. Stereotypes are wrong—most homeless people fly under the radar.

If the word "homeless" brings to mind a scruffy man with layers of clothing, holding a piece of cardboard, panhandling, then you need a reality check. This stereotypical image is not always accurate, and in no way does it represent the vast majority of homeless people in America.

In fact, families are the fastest growing segment of the homeless population. Most of these families are led by a single mother with two or three children. Yes, that's right—children. One study found that one in 50 children in America faces homelessness each year (according to the homeless definition used by schools, although this is a topic often debated among homeless advocates).

So why does this stereotypical image persist when the reality of homelessness is so different? Because we can't see it. Because it's not as easy a story to put on the front page of the papers. And because poverty and inequality are not sexy, exciting topics.

Which brings us to...

5. Get mad; mad enough to do something.

Do you think it's unacceptable that we live in a country where people are forced to sleep on the streets, scrape to make ends meet, and choose between medical care and paying rent? Then congratulations, **you are now a homeless advocate!**

This is a responsibility you should not take lightly, as hundreds of thousands of people will likely experience homelessness in the coming year. These people, and those who are on the brink of homelessness, need people like you who understand the issue and are willing to do something about it.

To get you started in this new role, take a look at your own community. Find out if homeless people's immediate needs are being met and if a long-term plan is in place to eradicate homelessness. Ask questions. Dispel antiquated myths and stereotypes and take advantage of opportunities to enlighten others about the modern-day realities of homelessness. Read up. Follow the news. Stay informed.

Most importantly, understand that homelessness is not a stigma or an indication of personal shortcomings. Rather, it is simply the state of not having a home in which to live.

Shannon writes for Change.org's End Homelessness blog. She has worked in homeless shelters and service organizations in San Francisco, the Triangle region of North Carolina and currently in the greater Boston area. She is a graduate student studying housing and urban policy at Tufts University.

Web: Homelessness.Change.org
Twitter: @EndHomelessness

Mark

Detroit

"It's a never ending battle out here," Mark says. He struggles to avoid the weather, find food and stay safe. He was robbed a few months ago and lost everything, including his ID.

He has trouble getting a job, thanks to a few felonies on his record—nobody will give him a second chance. He stays in Michigan because it's where he was born.

"[I'm] just out here surviving every day," Mark says. "You gotta do what you gotta do."

He slept outside last night and survives on church food pantries and donated meals.

Three wishes:

1. Get out of this situation.
2. A roof over his head—a home of his own so he could be warm.
3. An income.

http://invisiblepeople.tv/blog/2009/12/mark-homeless-detroit/

Hero

by Brandon Mendelson

There are few who deserve the title of "Hero." Mark Horvath is one of them.

This book is full of reasons why, but I won't get into that here.

Instead, I want to tell you about how Mark serves as a symbol of hope for America's homeless.

Young or old. Man or woman. Mark was one of them. He knows the story. He knows the struggle. Through sheer force of will Mark has undergone a resurrection that is possible for each and every one of them. They just need someone to look to, not cheap words or pity.

Mark is that person. Through his efforts in giving a voice to the voiceless, we know their story. We know the challenges they face. And through Mark, we know that this is not the end for them, but a beginning. One brought about by Mark's example.

The world is a better place for his existence on this earth. Thanks to Mark's efforts and the optimism and renewed spirit he brings to America's homeless, together we step closer to ending the homeless crisis in America.

Brandon Mendelson is the co-author of *Dracula And Kittens*.

Web: BrandonMendelson.com
Twitter: @BJMendelson

Cecilia

San Luis Obispo, Calif.

"I put a smile on my face for my kids' sake," says Cecilia. "My biggest challenge is to be a successful mother." As a homeless, single mom, she does her best to stay positive.

Each morning Cecilia and her children must vacate the evening-only shelter. Her 9-year-old son heads off to school while Cecilia and her 3-year-old daughter Juliana go to a center where they can spend the day. At 3 p.m. the day center closes, so they head to a park to kill time before returning to the evening shelter. Then they wait two hours in line for a bed.

"People could help by finding out the background and information about the real person," Cecilia says. "[We] are not a statistic."

Cecilia lost her house two years ago and has been homeless since. She's trying to save up enough to get a place to stay, but it's hard and happens slowly.

"It's very hard—that's why it's taking longer than I expected it to," Cecilia says. "I blocked out the bad. I'd probably get sick if I dwelled on the bad. I'm a very cheerful person."

Three Wishes:

1. A home for her kids.
2. Good health.
3. Be happy.

http://invisiblepeople.tv/blog/2009/04/cecilia-and-juliana/

Misconception #1: The Smelly, Dirty Homeless

All homeless people are the stereotypical dirty, smelly, mentally unstable, alcoholics that you see at the exit ramp or under an overpass.

Not true. Families are homeless. Children are homeless. Babies are homeless. In fact, children account for nearly 40 percent of the homeless population in the United States.[1] Families with children are the fastest growing segment of the homeless population—and those numbers are all pre-recession.

The stereotypical image of a homeless person is often what's considered chronic homelessness. In reality, 80 percent of the homeless find themselves in that situation temporarily.[2] These are families, moms and dads, trying to provide for their kids and for whatever reason their options ran out. They had nowhere else to go. Forget the statistics and spend some time at InvisiblePeople.tv hearing their stories. You can hear the desperation in their voices.

This is the true voice of homelessness. It's not the raspy holler of the drunk on the corner asking for a handout, though he could use some help too.

We're talking about the voice of families. People with kids who have come to the end of their rope. An emergency strikes and they find themselves out on the streets. In many cases they bounce in and out of homelessness as one situation deteriorates and they just can't build up enough of a reserve to survive the next crisis. Some families have bounced around the country from job to job, last chance effort to last chance effort, and now find themselves in a new city with no friends or family to turn to. They end up in shelters.

So before you write off the homeless as the drunk on the corner or the guy in the park who talks to himself, remember that moms and dads, children and babies are homeless too.

---

1   http://www.nationalhomeless.org/factsheets/who.html
2   http://www.gladwell.com/2006/2006_02_13_a_murray.html

Gypsy

Des Moines, Iowa

What's it like being a homeless mom? "It's really hard," says Gypsy.

She has two boys, a 10-year-old and a 3-year-old. Both have been sleeping with a friend for the past two months. The 10-year-old is in school all day and she only sees him for five minutes a day. She gets to spend the day with her other son, but there's not much to do with a 3-year-old when you're homeless.

"Today we missed the free feeding because I had an appointment, so he's hungry," Gypsy says. But her friend will feed him tonight. Meanwhile Gypsy will have to get food from another meal service tonight.

A local church graciously purchased bus tickets so Gypsy and her boys can return home to Arizona in a few weeks.

Three Wishes:

1. Her children to be successful.
2. The friends she's made out here could do something with their lives and get off the streets.
3. After two wishes for others, she couldn't think of a third.

http://invisiblepeople.tv/blog/2010/02/gypsy-homeless-family-iowa/

Compassion vs. Comparison

by Jeff Lilley

Maurice came walking down the street in his socks. It was just past midnight, and the streets of Seattle were wet and cold. I was out with our search and rescue van delivering hot chocolate, blankets, hats, gloves, sandwiches and socks. We asked if he wanted some hot chocolate.

"Do you have any shoes?" Maurice asked.

We looked down at his feet (big feet).

"What size do you wear?" We didn't have any shoes to give away, so the question was really pointless.

"Thirteen," he said.

This is where I was confronted by the shallowness of my value system. The Bible says if a man asks for your shirt, give him your coat also. Here we're out in the city specifically to give clothing and food to the needy, and the needy expressed their need. In fact, I could see his need as he walked toward me.

He needs shoes. I have shoes. But I can't just give away my shoes. What will I wear? What if my feet get wet? How do I explain this to my wife?

Does it matter that I own at least five pairs of shoes? Does it matter that we are on our last stop of the night and then headed home? Does it matter that I even have a pair of shoes back at the mission I could wear home? Does it matter that I am hesitant to give when confronted with a real, legitimate need?

That night I was confronted with who I was. When I met Maurice, I was trying to meet the needs of the homeless, trying to show compassion. But I've learned my primary response is rarely true compassion.

I've avoided the issue of homelessness in almost the same manner as I have avoided those who are actually homeless. At freeway off-ramps standing two feet away holding a piece of cardboard, I've told myself that any money I gave them will likely be spent on alcohol or drugs.

Attaching stereotypes and bias (however accurate it may be), I quickly compare. I think about how fortunate I am to be in my car, to have a place to call home, to have a job. In the process I no longer see them standing just outside my car window.

If he is an addict, shouldn't that break my heart just as much? Shouldn't I ache with the fact that he has a family that hurts for him and his choices? Shouldn't I look him in the eye and realize that avoiding him may be the very response that created his broken life in the first place?

When confronted with another's hurt, misfortune, addictions or mental illness, I typically focus on my own good fortune. I walk away feeling better about myself because: "At least I'm not like them."

That's not compassion. It is comparison.

After nearly three decades of working with youth in the mountains of California, Jeff Lilley is now the president of Seattle's Union Gospel Mission. Jeff, and his wife Eugenie, have five children, six grandchildren and one cat.

Web: ugm.org

Elvin

Baton Rouge, La.

"I shouldn't have to live like this," says Elvin. He has a degree in political science and worked for 20 years as a nurse. He's been homeless for a year and lives under a bridge.

"I had it all and I ended up on the streets," Elvin says. "A lot of people don't realize that anyone could end up where I am."

Elvin was married for 25 years and has three kids.

"Life sometimes deals you some bad cards and you have to play them," says Elvin. Right now he's working to renew his nursing license and get back to work.

If nothing else he hopes his children learn from his experience.

"You gotta get back up," Elvin says. "I did my down time. It's time to get back up now."

Three Wishes:

1. Never ended his marriage.
2. His children (Elvin never wished for anything specific, he just talked about his three grown children).
3. Get back to where he was.

http://invisiblepeople.tv/blog/2009/08/elvin-homeless-baton-rouge/

Who Is This Crazy Guy?

by Heather Meeker

I'll never forget the moment I first met Mark Horvath. The company I work for (Pelago, makers of Whrrl) had just launched the second generation of our product. I was at my home office in Los Angeles checking out the Twitter stream of Whrrl updates. After all, we did just launch, and I was super excited to see who was using our product.

Then it happened. I noticed a tweet from a man named @hardlynormal about strolling into a homeless camp. At the same time my Seattle-based co-workers sent me an e-mail: "Did you see that crazy guy walking into a homeless camp?" What?

I was intrigued and wanted to learn more. Sure enough, @hardlynormal was telling a story from a tent city consisting of homeless individuals in Sacramento, Calif.—the same place Oprah had television crews visit months earlier. Now, Mark was going up to some of these same people, who weren't too excited to see him after the Oprah expose.

The next update read: "I'm going in." Stereotypes of homeless people flooded my mind. I wasn't so sure I'd be that eager to waltz into a homeless encampment by myself. I followed along as he updated his story with pictures and notes. The next update was a picture of a homeless man, someone who had lost their house and job and, well, everything. Their story was coming across our little application, thanks to this man who goes by "Hardly Normal."

And this was the start of my relationship with the man who I later came to know as Mark Horvath. A man who was formerly homeless himself and is now dedicated to telling stories of homelessness around the nation. A man who was now facing homelessness—again—after losing his job due to the economy. A man who had a laptop, an iPhone and social media to tell stories of the forgotten people. A man with a mission.

Months passed as I learned more about InvisiblePeople.tv, kept up with Mark's daily tweets from the streets and watched the stories unfold. I decided Mark was crazy in the best way possible, so I had to meet him. We convened at the Dream Center in downtown Los Angeles and headed to skid row to do what else—hand out socks—a valuable commodity to those on the street. That was the day Mark told me of his dream to travel the nation and tell stories from the road. I'm proud to say Whrrl helped kick start that dream and I was able to be a part of it.

Through the power of social media, Mark has helped me to look at homelessness in a whole new way—with compassion. Some choose life on the streets, but many do not. Like the woman who left her abusive husband. The child who lost her parents. Or the family that lost their home to foreclosure. Mark has opened my eyes to not just pass by the person on the street, but to consider for one moment the story behind their situation.

Heather Meeker is a seasoned communications executive. She has worked for several Internet companies in various PR and marketing roles, including EarthLink, Yahoo!, Move.com and Stamps.com. Meeker briefly sold drugs (legally) at Pfizer but today heads up corporate communications and marketing for Pelago, makers of Whrrl.

Web: BloggedAmbition.com
Twitter: @heathermeeker

Coreen

Seattle

Coreen is waking up to her first morning as a resident of Nickelsville, a tent city in Seattle. She ran away from home at 5 a.m. the previous day to escape an abusive and violent relationship.

"[Homelessness] is pretty scary," Coreen says, "But it's better than what I was in."

She is happy to have found a community like Nickelsville. Coreen's first night in the tent city was the best night's sleep she's had in over a year, because now she feels safe.

Three Wishes:

    1. A job.
    2. A place to live.
    3. Feel safe.

http://invisiblepeople.tv/blog/2009/09/coreen-homeless-ten-city-seattle-nickelsville/

Drew

St. Petersburg, Fla.

"I lost track of my life," says Drew. He lost his job as a welder thanks to the economy. Then a drunk driver killed his family. He has a bachelor's degree in fire science and was working on a civil engineering degree. He's a structural certified welder, but nobody is hiring.

"It could happen that quick to anybody," Drew says, "So you probably shouldn't judge the next time you see somebody asking for just a little bit of help."

Drew has been homeless for four months. He survives by eating food he finds in dumpsters.

Three Wishes:

1. People would help each other and stop killing each other.
2. Get his family back.
3. Understand why things happen.

http://invisiblepeople.tv/blog/2009/08/drew-homeless-tampa-florid/

Open Our Eyes: Seeing the Invisible People of Homelessness

Misconception #2: It's Their Own Fault

If someone ended up on the street it's their own fault and they deserve whatever they get. It's not my problem.

Another standard excuse is that being homeless is their own fault. It's their mess, they can fix it. And in some cases it is true that poor choices have landed a person on the street. But in so many more cases circumstances conspired against someone. They lost a job through no fault of their own or bills piled up from an accident or they lost their health—so many things beyond our control can ruin our seemingly perfect life.

A substantial percentage of the working population in the United States is only a few paychecks away from being homeless. All it may take is a single crisis and whatever safety net you had is gone. You could be one crisis away from sleeping in your car.

When that reality sinks in it becomes clear that we all need help. We can all be victims of circumstance and we shouldn't hold that against anyone.

Even if it is their own fault, people still deserve help. It doesn't matter whose fault it is. We're a nation that gives free legal defense to murderers—yet if someone's troubles are their own fault we won't help? People need and deserve second and third chances.

And if compassion won't motivate you, perhaps practicality will. Homelessness costs everyone money. Taxpayers end up footing the bill, so in the end, it is your problem.

James

Seattle

James is a community architect, but today he is building a kitchen table out of shipping pallets for a tent city in Seattle known as Nickelsville. For him, it's not a tent city, but a community.

"Here you have somewhere safe to sleep and a shared meal," he says. "The shelters downtown are already full." He's thankful for the family atmosphere at Nickelsville. Otherwise he'd be sleeping under a bridge.

"We are common people, too," James says. "Good people have made bad choices and the economy's in crisis."

James came to Seattle four months ago looking for work. The day after sharing his story James found a job as a forklift operator.

Thee Wishes

1. Everybody would get a permanent place to live.
2. Homeless people could come together to form a community.
3. Get out to Alaska to be a fish processor.

http://invisiblepeople.tv/blog/2009/06/james-homeless-nickelsville-seattle/

The Drive to Succeed

by Scott Monty

On the face of it, you really wouldn't expect a car company to be involved in a project regarding homelessness. Some might think the only connection is that some people who lose their homes end up sleeping in their vehicles. But Mark Horvath helped us at Ford Motor Company see that it's much deeper than that.

Since the very earliest days of Ford, we've been committed to giving back to the communities in which we do business; it's a strategic imperative that we contribute to a better world. And as a global manufacturer with a footprint on six continents and 120 countries, that's quite a bit of community involvement. While a lot of these initiatives may have nationwide visibility, we find that when our employees volunteer during Accelerated Action Days in local communities, they volunteer where they feel the most emotionally connected.

One of those connections comes into play in our involvement with Habitat for Humanity, where we're providing people power to build homes for those who need them. We don't do it with a lot of fanfare or because it helps our corporate reputation. We've committed to Habitat because it's something we believe in. When you look at what Mark did with InvisiblePeople.tv, it was his own version of our Accelerated Action Days—but he continued day in and day out and in a multitude of communities across the country.

While it takes stamina and fortitude to volunteer to help build homes for the homeless, for most people it's just a daylong or weeklong commitment. Mark has made us realize that homelessness is something that thousands of individuals have to endure every day, for weeks, months and even years at a time. Personally, I hadn't given much thought to homelessness before Mark put it on my radar. But now, because he's done it in such a human way—because he's made these people visible—his efforts will be long remembered and have a much deeper impact than most.

Scott Monty is the global head of social media for Ford Motor Company. As a member of the communications leadership team, he has helped shape the social media strategy of Ford. Scott's career has centered on strategic advisory work with a variety of clientele since he earned his MBA 15 years ago.

Web: ScottMonty.com
Twitter: @ScottMonty

Joni

New York

"Terrible things happen out here," says Joni, fighting back tears. "Especially to a woman." Last night she spent the night on a bench in Times Square, one of too many forgettable nights in the fours years she's been homeless.

"It's hard to get food," Joni says. "People always think you want money for drugs—which is not true. You want money to eat, to survive, to be able to walk. Just like me, right now, I can hardly walk I'm so weak."

She talks about the dangerous situation, being robbed and seeing people the next day with her stolen belongs.

"It's terrible," she says. "Somebody's gotta do something about it. There's too many people out here."

Three Wishes:

1. A home.
2. Wake up with food.
3. An end to homelessness.

http://invisiblepeople.tv/blog/2009/10/joni-homeless-times-square-new-york-city/

Social Media for Social Change

by Natalie Profant Komuro

We think we know who they are—the people with weathered faces, tattered belongings tied to a cart or strapped to their backs. They are everywhere in America, but for all their presence, they are anonymous and invisible. In 2008, capitalizing on the latest trends in video posting and online social media, Mark Horvath set out to bring them into full view. InvisiblePeople.tv introduces us to the men and women who have long been assigned stereotypes and dismissed from mainstream America. Their stories convey the pain, frustration and loss experienced by people who become homeless, as much as they reveal how woefully inadequate our public and private responses have been. And InvisiblePeople.tv doesn't leave it there.

With its unedited interviews of people living on the streets, InvisiblePeople.tv has accomplished something that no other group or individual in homeless advocacy has done. It has brought homeless people into our own homes without judgment or sanitizing their stories. In the frank, but respectful interviews people who have become accustomed to being ignored open up about their experiences. We see them at close range and hear in their own voice people we would otherwise pass on the streets or never notice because they have become so adept at removing themselves from view. Some interviews, like Paul in New York, bring a wry smile, as if we are listening to a well-worn blues song. Others, such as Joni's tearful remarks, are heart wrenching. Throughout these stories, there is the common refrain—that we, the housed, can and must do something. And if there is any doubt about Mark's intentions, one need only follow him on Twitter or Facebook where he ceaselessly exhorts his followers to take action.

InvisiblePeople.tv also connects those of us who are currently helping homeless people. Too often, providers of services for the homeless can become isolated because the daily demands of our work can be overwhelming. Web-based resources and social media sites can help us build and strengthen connections to support our work. This has been particularly true for newly formed efforts such as Help a Mother Out, which organizes diaper drives for social service agencies.

Contemporary homelessness, what we have seen persistently growing since the 1980s, has ebbed and flowed in its "popularity." Advocates have struggled over the years to push homelessness to the forefront of the national agenda, but never has it quite arrived. In our own communities committed professionals and volunteers do what they can, but the issue has not earned a sustained status. My hope is that InvisiblePeople.tv, by making the story so personal and relatable, will support, stimulate and provoke a new wave of engagement and activism that can once and for all, make the invisible visible and lead to meaningful solutions.

Natalie Profant Komuro, executive director of PATH Achieve Glendale, has worked in homeless services since 1987. Serving as director of policy and planning for the Los Angeles Homeless Services Authority from 1998-2007, she was elected co-chair of the National Shelter Plus Care Coalition in 2003. She received her master's in urban planning from UCLA.

Web: AchieveGlendale.org
Twitter: @anacapa

Jennifer

Los Angeles

Jennifer has lived on Skid Row for four years and she's never seen anything like it.

"It's hard, but life is what you make it," she says.

She came here addicted to drugs. She managed to go 13 months sober but then relapsed on Christmas Day. Now she's been sober for three months.

"I want to be a drug counselor," Jennifer says. "I want to be able to help people, show them how good recovery can actually be."

She sleeps in a tent on one of the side streets. She has a boyfriend to watch over her, so she knows she's safe at night.

"My lifelong goal is to be a writer, I've been wanting to be a writer since I was 8 years old," Jennifer says. "I write poetry."

Three Wishes:

1. Be able to have kids again.
2. To be married.
3. To have a house free of expenses.

http://invisiblepeople.tv/blog/2009/06/jennifer-homeless-skidrow/

Compassion Bridges Divides

by Stephanie Rudat

There is greatness in everyone. It may be boldly evident or nearly impossible to identify, but it is undoubtedly there. Often it's a matter of courageously unlocking the vault to the character deep within us and purposefully bringing it to the surface. This character has been constructed by the vast array of colors collected in our life's journey. The ups and downs from joys, anguish, successes, failures, triumphs and adversities all shape our character. Our greatness perseveres despite pressures while brightly reflecting our core values. It continues to support us, and those affected by our actions, as we inevitably experience the ups and downs of life.

Ups and downs are reflected everywhere. High tide washes footprints left behind in the sand. Storms bring snow that, in time, melts away. Earthquakes forge mountains and create valleys. Precious babies are born and loved ones pass on. Transitions bring colors to our character as our lives unfold. Loneliness delivers reflection. Fear fosters courage. Closed doors can inspire new ones to open. Meeting a stranger is making a friend. Getting lost can lead to discovering a new way. Like our hearts beat, living is comprised of ups and downs. Without them, there's a flat line. Without them, we do not evolve into our greatness.

Our greatness breeds strength and acceptance of ourselves and others. It's in our hands that pull us from the depths of despair and are lent to others in need. It's in our vision that seeks the rainbow in a storm and identifies special characteristics in others. It is by maintaining faith that we can overcome challenges and manage our destiny. Greatness comes from choosing the high road even if it is the road less traveled. It's giving generously without expectation. It is forgiving and loving without condition. It is staying true to our principles and standing up for the values of others.

No one is entirely better or worse off; compassion bridges divides. Greatness is exemplified in Mark Horvath's work providing solutions to the enormous issue of homelessness while still offering refuge to one homeless man, woman, child or family at a time. Reflective of his greatness, Mark's affliction to transform the stigma associated with homelessness through InvisiblePeople.tv remains his focus despite facing his own potential homelessness—again. Embracing the colorful composition that has constructed his character, Mark leads by example lifting the lows of others with empowerment to thrive.

Greatness comes from serving as a pillar of strength when you feel like your own two feet can barely support yourself. Greatness happens when providing words of encouragement although you don't have the fortitude to mutter the same declaration in the mirror. Mark Horvath consciously unlocks his vault and chooses impact over ease. You, too, can choose the same. Helping others epitomizes greatness. Simply stated in the words of Pema Chodron, "We work on ourselves in order to help others, but also we help others in order to work on ourselves."

Stephanie Rudat is a principle-centered businesswoman and social entrepreneur. Reflective of her passions, she co-founded Alliance of Youth Movements which positively empowers leaders to effect nonviolent change by creating and promoting use of technological tools to advance freedom, human rights, democracy and civil society development around the world.

Web: StephanieRudat.Tumblr.com
Twitter: @SRudat

Tom

Fayetteville, Ark.

"I came home from work one day and the wife had left and taken everything," Tom says. "So I thought it was a real good idea to go out and get drunk. I missed my job the next day, got fired and got sucked up in this spiral right here called homelessness. That's about it."

Tom shrugs as he recounts the quick story that led to him being homeless for the past five years. It only took a month for him to end up here. Right now 'here' is a homeless encampment in the woods of Fayetteville, Ark.

"A rich, cultural, affluent town like this, you wouldn't think there'd be a lot of homeless people," Tom says. "But I can show you camp after camp after camp."

Tom sees homelessness as a cycle that's nearly impossible to break out of. You become dependent on people for food, you try to find a place to stay and get arrested and fined. Nothing goes right.

"It's a never ending battle. It gets depressing sometimes," Tom says. But then he straightens up and refuses to give in: "Never give up. Never give up."

Three Wishes:

1. Shelter.
2. Become mobile.
3. Friends stay safe.

http://invisiblepeople.tv/blog/2009/07/tom-homeless-arkansas/

We're All in This Together

by Becky Kanis

I remember the first time I asked someone living on the streets if I could take their picture. It was the summer of 2004 and the Republican Convention was coming to Madison Square Garden. At the time, 50 people had made the Amtrak and subway stations their home. The city insisted that it had humanely relocated everyone to shelter prior to the coming security sweeps. Our team went through Penn Station to document the fact that, indeed, many people remained behind and were at risk for harsh treatment.

I remember easy conversations with people who were more than happy to have their picture taken, jokes about wanting to fix up their hair or make sure that I "got their good side." Taking a picture of someone can be a way of connecting—it can remind us of our shared humanity.

What surprised me was the bureaucrat's response when I showed up with the photographs. She was livid. She went on a civil libertarian rant: "How dare you take their pictures?!" I responded, "A tourist could take their picture and no one would care. I take their picture to try to help them, and *now* you're worried about their rights?" Her discomfort with the pictures, in stark contrast to the comfort of the people living on the streets with having their picture taken, let me know that I was onto something.

Since then, New York City has completely changed their approach to outreach and housing placement to adopt the Street to Home model. Getting to know each person, including taking their picture, was integrated into outreach procedures. Now, 100 people are placed from the streets into their own apartments each month and homelessness is down 47%.

As part of the 100,000 Homes Campaign, communities across the country are adapting the Street to Home model and the Vulnerability Index—a way of methodically canvassing the streets and ranking people for housing based on how long they've been homeless and the fragility of their health. Volunteers go out at 4 a.m. to help outreach teams identify every person sleeping outside, getting their name, photograph and health conditions. The degree of specificity and the urgency of the health conditions helps move communities to action.

Open Our Eyes: Seeing the Invisible People of Homelessness

So far over 3,500 of the most vulnerable people in the country have received housing and health care.

With homelessness, anonymity is death. Homelessness has a mortality rate on par with some cancers. With every picture we take, we strip away that anonymity, we begin to restore a connection and we help people who would much rather avert their eyes to look homelessness in the face. Once you see homelessness in a personal way, you have to do something about it. That is what InvisiblePeople.tv is all about to me: It's another way to remind us that we are not so different, that we are all connected, that we are all in this together.

Becky Kanis directs the 100,000 Homes Campaign for Common Ground—a movement to help communities identify and house their most chronic and vulnerable homeless. She helps volunteers across the country hit the streets at 4 a.m. to know each person living outside by name, photograph and mortality risk.

Twitter: @beckykanis

Brianna

Wal-Mart Parking Lot in California

"I'm not sleeping face down on the concrete like so many are," says Brianna. "So I'm really lucky." Instead the 24-year-old sleeps in a borrowed trailer in a Wal-Mart parking lot. Brianna's been homeless for 12 days and lost her job as an executive assistant eight months ago. It's the first time she's been unemployed since she started working as a 12-year-old to help support her family.

"It's crazy how many people like me are out there," she says. Brianna is a member of the largest demographic of homeless, the mobile homeless. However, she stays positive and is thankful for her trailer, laptop and pet dog.

"The biggest challenge is staying positive," Brianna says. "It's OK to be depressed about it sometimes. You panic, let the panic run its course and get back to the objective—stay safe and reverse this thing."

For Brianna, that's already happening. Yesterday she got a job. "But I'm still homeless," she says, reflecting on the new challenges of holding down a job without a place to live.

"This could happen to anyone. I don't care if you're a CEO or a janitor," Brianna says. "We're all just one step away, one foreclosure away, one paycheck away, one family argument away. That's the biggest thing I've learned—never say this couldn't happen to me."

Brianna started her own blog as a way to make light of a serious situation—GirlsGuideToHomelessness.com. As the blog gained exposure and attention it's turned into a tool to help turn her situation around. In 2009 *Elle* magazine made headlines when they hired Brianna for a low paid internship. She landed a book deal at the end of 2009.

Three wishes:

1. Buy and renovate a historic home.

2. Her friend Matt could get the word out about homelessness.

3. Economy could correct itself.

http://invisiblepeople.tv/blog/2009/03/brianna/

Open Our Eyes: Seeing the Invisible People of Homelessness

Misconception #3: Lazy

Homeless people are just lazy.

It's a common misconception about homelessness and honestly it's pretty easy to come to that conclusion. If you see a homeless person sitting around in a park all day you might begin to wonder what they're doing. But laziness generally has nothing to do with it. It's more about being crushed by an impossible system and a loss of hope.

Imagine for a moment that you're homeless. You have no job, no home, no bank account—nothing. You need to get to a social service agency to get some help, but you have no car so you have to beg for some bus fair just to get there. Two transfers and an hour and a half later you're sitting in the lobby filling out paperwork. You filled out the same paperwork at a different agency yesterday, but now you're doing it all again. Then you wait. All day. After hours of waiting they explain that you don't qualify or the program is full or that you'll be added to a waiting list—pick the excuse, but that's likely what you'll hear because social service agencies have too many people to serve and not enough resources. If you're lucky they'll offer you a bus pass to get home ('home' being the park or bench or overpass where you've found shelter). At the end of the day you're still out of luck. Still homeless, still hungry, still broke. Tomorrow you'll repeat the process, and you'll do it again the next day and the next, until you get the help you need or you finally give up.

Navigating the bureaucracy of the social services system is a nightmare. Mark Horvath often remarks that he has two cell phones a laptop, a car and he works in the social services industry and he still can't navigate the system. If he can't do it, how is someone living in a park with no resources going to be able to do it?

After a while it's not surprising that people throw their hands up and accept their hopelessness. Suddenly sitting around in a park all day doesn't sound so bad. Those people you see aren't lazy—they've been crushed by an inhumane system and lost all hope.

Eddie

Binghamton, N.Y.

"[People] look at you like you're nothing but a piece of garbage," says Eddie. He collects cans and bottles as a source of income. Since his tent and sleeping bag were stolen, he uses whatever blankets he can find to sleep through the sub-freezing nights. Last night he couldn't sleep because his feet were so cold they hurt.

He is a homeless man in a town of approximately 45,000 people. The only cold weather shelter is reserved for alcoholics and is usually full. He says it takes 45 days for the department of social services to do anything, and then you need an address and an ID.

Eddie is a short order cook by trade, but now he wears a brace so it's hard to get a job.

"I'm hoping I can survive another day," Eddie says. "That's my future."

Three wishes:

1. Get back with his girl.
2. Get back with his kids.
3. Open a homeless shelter in Binghamton.

http://invisiblepeople.tv/blog/2009/03/eddie/

Palliative Care for Those Living in Poverty?

by Alan Graham

Palliative care (from Latin *palliare,* to cloak) is any form of medical care or treatment that concentrates on reducing the severity of disease symptoms, rather than striving to halt, delay or reverse progression of the disease itself or provide a cure. The goal is to prevent and relieve suffering and to improve quality of life for people facing serious, complex illness.

The above definition comes from Wikipedia. The advent of the hospice movement in the United States and the creation of medical practices dedicated to palliative care are two of the most important events of the 20th century. These advances have actually had a dramatic and positive impact on medical care in not only how we treat patients but perhaps even more importantly how we treat those impacted by the patients' disease.

So what if we treat poverty as the disease that it is? And homelessness being the greatest manifestation of poverty here in the United States, what if we began to focus on relieving the suffering of the symptoms of that disease? What if just for a moment in time we took our eyes off of the cure and focused only on this issue of suffering? To relieve the extraordinary suffering associated with poverty! Imagine!

What would be the impact on those who suffer and on those who are impacted by their suffering? Wow! We could be really on to something here. Don't doubt for a second that the impoverished plight of the homeless, as an example, does not impact all of us living in the same community. The burden on the emergency rooms, the burden on the criminal justice system, the burden on our downtowns. If we begin to merely relieve their suffering would it relieve the suffering of the community as a whole? Relieve, that is, not solve?

Because I do not believe there are "solutions." It is really only caring for people that is the "solution." And I have seen it work. I have watched suffering human beings be lifted off of the streets then heal from the ravages of the streets and re-purpose their lives to be contributors to their community. I haven't seen poverty or homelessness solved, but I have seen suffering relieved!

Alan Graham is the president and founder of Mobile Loaves and Fishes, a social profit enterprise that delivers meals to homeless and working poor people on the streets of Austin, Texas; San Antonio; New Orleans; Nashville, Tenn.; Providence, R.I.; and Minneapolis.

Web: mlfnow.org
Twitter: @mlfnow

Jim

Las Vegas

It's 116 degrees and Jim is just trying to survive in a tent city on the side of a highway in Las Vegas. Jim has full blown AIDS and doesn't have access to the medical care he needs.

He came here from Los Angeles on a freight train hoping to get a fresh start. "But it didn't work," he says. "I got deeper in the hole." He's thankful for food stamps, but other assistance is hard to come by. Catholic Charities was offering some help, but their budget ran out. The city also tries to discourage homelessness by forcing the tent city to move. Jim has had to move eight times himself.

"It's hard on everybody, this recession," Jim says. "It's just a little more hard on the homeless."

Three Wishes

1. World peace.
2. Treat each other equal.
3. We would care for one another.

http://invisiblepeople.tv/blog/2009/07/jim-homeless-vegas

Reflections on Homelessness

by Jeff Holden

Homelessness is a large and insidious problem. The concept of humans, in this day and age, being reduced to living essentially like animals is deeply troubling, but its self-perpetuating properties amplify the pain: Once a person is homeless, barriers arise that prevent them from returning to a humane situation. For example, lack of regular access to a shower or reasonable place to sleep or a phone makes it very hard to have a successful job interview, which keeps the person unemployed and, therefore, without cash or credit, and so on.

What surprises me perhaps the most is how unsolved the problem continues to be. I don't fool myself that it's a simple problem to solve, but I do believe it *is* largely solvable. In part, I derive that belief from my own desire to help combined with the fact that I do much less to help than I theoretically could. In my case, that disconnect comes from there being no straightforward, clearly useful and leveraged way to help. I do not, for example, believe that handing out a few dollars at a time to individual homeless people is helpful in any important way.

If I'm in this conundrum, there must be many other people with means and desire to help without a suitable channel. In other words, there is strong supply and demand, but no efficient way to bring them together.

Now, in reading the above, one might think that I'm simply making excuses, i.e., that I'm merely lazy or otherwise unmotivated to find a channel by which I can help. Some of that is perhaps fair criticism, but what is true is that if there were an easily accessible and clearly "right" opportunity to help that was easily discoverable, I would jump on it. I feel certain this generalizes how a large number of people would also respond.

So this begs the question, what would a *good* solution look like?

First and foremost, it would resolve the *root causes* of the homelessness, not simply ease the symptoms. There are many reasons whereby people become homeless—sudden loss of income, poor management of finances, a death of the key provider in the family, mental illness, fleeing domestic abuse and others—but the root cause of their *remaining* homeless needs to be the focus. (I should add that truly solving homelessness should start far upstream, during the formative years, with education and strong guidance. This is the subject of a much longer discussion, but programs like SummerSearch.org are a shining light in this regard.)

Secondly, I deeply believe in the concept of empowering self-sufficiency, as opposed to simple welfare or subsidy models, the latter of which can actually motivate behaviors optimized for maintaining or increasing the subsidy rather than escaping the situation. Furthermore, the psychological effects that come from controlling one's own destiny cannot be overstated, and such an approach also leverages the productivity of the very people who need the help, driving costs down.

While my searches for existing programs that exemplify these principles have been rather disappointing, one proposal, by urban designer Michael E. Arth, called Villages for the Homeless (VillagesfortheHomeless.org) is rather exciting. It is gaining sufficient momentum that it looks likely to come to fruition. It will be a fabulous social experiment that can be replicated widely if successful. In addition to my rather feeble local contributions to the cause, I certainly intend to support it.

Jeff Holden, founder/CEO of Pelago, Inc., is a computer scientist, fascinated by the intersection of the physical and virtual worlds. Pelago created Whrrl, a mobile location-based product enabling people to explore and experience their cities in an entirely new way. Prior, Jeff was a senior VP at Amazon.com.

Web: Whrrl.com
Twitter: @JeffHolden

Mark

Phoenix

"I lost my job, lost my apartment. It could happen to anybody, I guess," Mark says with a shrug. He's 22 and homeless. Last night he slept behind a bus stop.

"Every day I look for a job," he says. He starts walking in one direction and applies everywhere he can. But these days a lot of places aren't even taking applications. He's been homeless for four months now, but he's been homeless off and on for a long time.

"I survive by the grace of God," Mark says, "Like anybody else."

Three Wishes:

1. "I want a job. That's it."

http://invisiblepeople.tv/blog/2009/02/mark-2/

Misconception #4: Get a Job

Why don't homeless people just get a job?

Get a job. That's another common misconception about homeless people. Many of the people Mark Horvath has talked to would love to have a job. Unfortunately, it's not as simple as it sounds.

First of all, the job market is horrible. Seven million people were laid off in 2009, making the competition for the few jobs available fierce.

As if that competition and the bleak job market weren't enough, homeless people face their own unique set of obstacles. Every job application asks for a phone number and a mailing address. You can't just put the street where you park and sleep in your car. Every job interview is going to require dressing your best and looking professional. Good luck getting the wrinkles out of your shirt or finding time to shower when you sleep on a bench. You probably know plenty of people with a house, a car, a vast selection of professional attire, a phone and everything else and they still have a hard time finding a job. Imagine doing it without all of those basic necessities.

And landing the job is only half the battle. Once you get that job, you have to keep it. Being on time and looking professional is a challenge when you don't have housing, clean clothes, easy access to a shower, convenient transportation or the likelihood of a good night's sleep. That first paycheck won't come for a couple weeks, so even if you land a job, your situation won't change for a while. And to make it worse, now you're working in that coveted job, so the soup kitchen that's been keeping you fed might be closed by the time you get off work. You landed a job, but now you're starving.

Unfortunately, the cards are stacked against a homeless person finding a job.

Tony

Los Angeles

Tony panhandles at a freeway exit ramp with a cardboard sign that reads "Homeless Vet." He had a job but got laid off and hasn't been able to find work. He does maintenance work when he can get it but has had to turn to panhandling to survive.

"People holler, 'Get a job,'" Tony says, "Put them in my shoes and let's see how they feel."

"Don't get me wrong, I do try to get a job," he explains. "But it's not really easy. In the time being you have to have some way to survive." He uses the money from panhandling to pay for food, clothes and the occasional night in a motel. Normally he sleeps in a sleeping bag in the nearby hills.

"You can stand out here for five to six hours and you might make three bucks," Tony says. He admits to a drug addiction and says he used to support his habit with panhandling, but now he's fighting the addiction and staying sober.

Tony served in the U.S. Marine Corps and comments that there are a lot of homeless veterans on the streets. People tell him to go to the VA office, but he says it takes too long. "If I wait for the government to take care of me, I'll probably be dead by the time I receive something," Tony says.

"I know that I'm a better person and I can do better than this," Tony says. "But the economy is so tight..." He trails off. He is hopeful about a job lead, but until then he'll be at the exit ramp panhandling to make ends meet.

Three wishes:

1. Have an apartment.
2. Good job.
3. Be a cook.

http://invisiblepeople.tv/blog/2009/04/tony/

Nathan

Portland

As the rain beats down on Nathan's face, he tells his story: "I have been homeless off and on since I was about 10 and steadily since I was 15."

He went to a transitional housing program in his late teens, but ended up back on the streets.

"This time I'm homeless because my ceiling fell in," says Nathan, 27. The roof of his girlfriend's apartment caved in after heavy rains, leaving them with nowhere to stay.

He tries to find dry places to sleep or at the very least awnings where he is allowed to get shelter from the rain. He survives with a sleeping bag and a few jackets to stay warm.

Three Wishes:

1. A car or a van that he can transform into a mobile home.
2. A job.
3. Mostly a job.

http://invisiblepeople.tv/blog/2009/11/nathan-homeless-portland-oregon/

Conversations and a Cup of Coffee

by Michael Ian

Like many folks, I have a morning routine to start my day. It includes a visit to Starbucks for a cup of coffee. Most of the folks who arrive around the same time are regulars and are known to the baristas by name—as well as by their choice of morning beverage.

One gentleman, who I sit and speak with for about 30 minutes, is a kindly person. However, like so many Americans, he has become a victim of the nation's current economic woes. Furthermore, he has become one of a growing number of Americans who are seldom recognized as being in financial crisis: the under-employed.

Over the last six months or so, in order to stay afloat, the company he has worked for over the last 21 years has had to lay off some of its workers. Those who have been kept have had their work hours cut dramatically. Most recently, workers have worked four days one week, and three days the following week, and so on, in alternating cycles.

This week, the company has been closed altogether. And some employees have been contacted and told not to report for work next week.

This gentleman knows that I blog about homelessness. As a result, these last two or three weeks he has been asking me (in a round about manner) what types of homeless resources are available in our small community. In particular, he has asked about shelter facilities for homeless families.

Although he has tried to make his inquires seem casual, I can sense his underlying concern that he and his family may soon end up homeless.

It has been troubling to note that his shoulders seem to have begun to sag under the weight of the stress and to see the near despair in his eyes. More than that, it has been heartrending to watch his sense of dignity erode.

He has never had any illusions about being wealthy.

His aspirations have been more humble: To earn enough to keep a roof over the heads of his small family, pay his bills on time, put away a few bucks each month, and perhaps even have something left over to order out for a pizza or go out to dinner every now and again.

This gentleman is a continued reminder of a truism that I have maintained for years: Homelessness can afflict anyone.

It is not a respecter of persons; their ethnicity; their gender or age group; their religious or theological beliefs; their political affiliations; or their educational backgrounds.

It is a socio-economic condition that occurs when a person or family can no longer afford to maintain housing of their own.

I hope this gentleman can weather the storm.

I have come to enjoy our conversations over our morning cup of coffee and will sorely miss them if he and his family become the next victims of homelessness—and, as a result, "invisible people" in the eyes of the rest of the community.

Michael Ian is the author of the SLO Homeless blog. He currently lives in central California.

Web: slohomeless.wordpress.com

Jody & Phillip

St. Paul, Minn.

Jody sold everything she had to buy a car—so she could live in it. That was her only choice after being unfairly evicted from her apartment. She lived in the car with her 19-year-old son Phillip, but it was too crowded and now she sleeps in the car and he sleeps in a shelter in downtown St. Paul.

Jody and Phillip have been homeless for two months. They struggle to get an apartment because Jody has felony convictions and a chunk of her disability check goes to pay child support.

Jody hopes her son can find a job. "He has been trying," she acknowledges. "But it's hard for him too, he has disabilities."

Three Wishes:

1. Job.

2. Apartment.

3. Car repairs.

http://invisiblepeople.tv/blog/2010/01/jody-and-phillip-homeless-youth-st-paul/

A New Era in Problem Solving

by Kari Saratovsky

With the economy still in uncharted territory and families struggling to make ends meet, we have watched as individuals have been forced to do more with less. No matter where you come from, the past year impacted individuals at every spectrum of the socio-economic ladder. If you weren't personally impacted by the economic downturn you certainly knew someone who was—be it a neighbor who lost her job, a relative who was having trouble putting food on the table or friends who were one paycheck away from losing their house.

Last fall, I had the opportunity to catch up with Mark Horvath as he made his way back to California following a cross-country road trip where he documented stories of the homeless through a series of powerful, raw and unedited videos that have forever changed my perception of homelessness in America.

What Mark helped me and countless others recognize is that homelessness is a growing issue, but it cannot be viewed in isolation. Hunger is a major problem here in the United States, and hunger is closely tied to poverty, and poverty is tied to homelessness, and homelessness is tied to access to education, and on and on.

Just as these issues are interconnected, we find ourselves living in a new and interconnected world. How we communicate and share information is rapidly changing. Information moves fast, and people are more closely connected in new and different ways.

All of this has shifted how we support causes and mobilize people to action—whether our cause is homelessness or environmental sustainability. At the same time, we are witnessing what many believe to be the beginning of a new era of problem solving and social entrepreneurship—we no longer look to one sector to help solve our most challenging social problems, but rather we see the power of blending sectors, structures and savvy entrepreneurs (like Mark), that will lead to meaningful impact.

What Mark has done to educate and inspire all of us is no small feat. Not only has he given a face to the invisible, but he reminds us that no matter what our passion, each of us has influence. It's what you choose to do with this influence that is truly powerful.

As vice president of social innovation at the Case Foundation, Kari is an evangelist for all things social media for social good. With experience in the government and nonprofit sectors, her favorite role is that of a connector—connecting passionate people, good ideas and new approaches in an effort to address social problems.

Web: SocialCitizens.org
Twitter: @SocialCitizen

David, Tish & Natasha

San Luis Obispo, Calif.

"Every day is a struggle," says David, who lives in a homeless shelter with his wife Tish and their 15-month-old daughter Natasha. "We don't have any place like home to go to, so we make the best of what we have and the services that are offered here."

Right now they're in the Prado Day Center in San Luis Obispo, Calif. They hope to get back on their feet and become a self-sufficient family.

"We try to be upbeat and help other people," David says. "When you help people, you get a lot of help back."

Both David and Tish are quick to point out that homelessness is not a disease. It's a situation that people fall into.

"We're homeless, we're not less human," says Tish. "Everybody is only one screwed up paycheck away from being right where we are."

"We're not looking for handouts or money or places to stay," says David. "Just a smile and treat us like normal people. We're just as normal as they are."

David and Tish are both former drug addicts and come from broken families. They're trying to put their lives back together and provide for their daughter, who is clearly the glue that holds them together.

"We're homeless, but we're happy and smiling today and that's because of our daughter," says David. "If we didn't have her I don't think we'd have the drive that we have to accomplish the things we want to accomplish."

Three Wishes:

1. For Natasha to grow up happy and healthy.
2. That she'd take advantage of every opportunity.
3. That she'd be happy with who she is.

http://invisiblepeople.tv/blog/2009/05/david-tish-and-natasha/

It Takes a Village

by Lisa Truong

The first time I witnessed family homelessness was in the early 1990s. I was working at a fly-by-night telecommunications company, located in China Basin Landing, in San Francisco. The ballpark hadn't been built and the SOMA warehouse district wasn't yet dotted with start-up companies. In this isolated area of the city it wasn't unusual to see lines of junky old RVs parked along Brannan or Third Streets.

A little girl, about 7 years old, came into the café I was at with her mom. Presumably, they lived in one of the vans or RVs parked nearby. The girl's blond hair was oily and tangled. She clearly needed a bath and change of clothes. They ordered a corndog and milk at the counter and sat at the table next to me. Her mom sat there as the girl ate her meal. And as I secretly stole glimpses of this family, I wondered about their situation. Why were they homeless? How come she wasn't in school? When was her last meal? Where was the father? I was concerned. I was judgmental. They left after they were finished. And I chose to look away.

Women and children are the fastest growing homeless population in America, according to the National Center on Family Homelessness. They are our "invisible homeless"—fleeing domestic violence, struggling with eviction and unemployment, couch surfing, living in weekly rate motels, out of their cars or in shelters. Homeless children experience high levels of trauma and stress, go hungry, and suffer from chronic and acute health problems. How can we say this doesn't matter to all of us?

For better or worse, our collective society raises our children. It takes a village to raise a child. Let's not look away.

Lisa Truong is co-founder and director of Help a Mother Out, a grassroots advocacy and direct action campaign. HAMO's mission is to help improve the lives of mothers, children and families in need one diaper at a time. She lives with her family in the San Francisco Bay Area.

Web: HelpAMotherOut.org
Twitter: @HelpAMotherOut

Jennifer

New York

Jennifer is six months pregnant and homeless on the streets of Manhattan. She came here from California with her husband.

"I got to panhandle to survive," she says. "To eat I go to churches, if they're open… I have to walk all over the place to find prenatal care."

Last night Jennifer and her husband slept on a mattress on the side of the street. At 5 a.m. the police woke them up and her husband was arrested for an old jay walking ticket.

She's applied to an assistance program and should have housing today. Long term she wants to go back to school

"I have to deal with it, go with the flow," Jennifer says. "Hopefully everything will work out the right way."

Three Wishes:

1. Housing.
2. Job for her husband.
3. "That's it," she says. "Money comes and goes, I don't really care if I have a whole lot of money or don't have any money, as long as I can be happy."

http://invisiblepeople.tv/blog/2009/04/jennifer/

Misconception #5: Panhandling for Subst

**Panhandling is a waste. They're either mi
enabling a drug or alcohol problem.**

Panhandling is a tricky one. How many me
showing panhandlers getting rich? The real

First and foremost, let's address the idea of dishonesty. It's a little bizarre that we put our complete trust in all kinds of people who manage our money—when so often those people are as corrupt and dishonest as they come. Remember Enron? The reality is the average American cheats on their taxes. And you're worried that the panhandler on the corner is going to put your 35 cents to some nefarious purpose?

Secondly, begging for money is humiliating. Have you ever had to ask your brother-in-law for a loan? It's no picnic. Now imagine standing at an exit ramp in dirty, smelly clothes, clutching a piece of cardboard and asking strangers for change. Some swear at you, others actually spit on you and so many refuse to even look at you, like you're an outcast or worse—invisible.

No one is asking for change because it's a good way to make a living. It sucks. You're a target, you're vulnerable and you're relying on whatever people decide to give you, which is rarely what you actually need. In many cases begging for money is the only way a homeless person can get the things they actually need—things like socks or a toothbrush.

It's true that some homeless people turn to drugs or alcohol to cope with the hardships of life—just like everybody else. We never ask this question of every other person we give our hard earned money to, from the tip jar at the coffee shop to the CEO of our bank, so why do we ask it of homeless people? Of all the dignities we deprive homeless people of, the loss of choice is perhaps the worst.

And for the record, if you had to use the side of the street as a toilet, you'd probably want a drink too.

Homeless people turn to panhandling because they have no other

Open Our Eyes: Seeing the Invisible People of Homelessness   67

tchens and food shelves might be plentiful, but try
othbrush, a bus pass, diapers or—let's get practical—

a world of choices they thought they'd never have to make,
panhandling is an option of last resort for a homeless person. So
have a little compassion and don't assume the worst.

Marco & Cherese

Southern California

"It is so humiliating to sit there and hold a sign saying 'Homeless: Need help'," says Cherese. She survives by holding up that sign at an intersection. Cherese and Marco are among the mobile homeless. They live in an RV on the side of the road.

"The average person will not know the humiliation of what it's like to hold a sign," says Marco. "Because they haven't been there." Recently Cherese was the victim of a hit-and-run at an exit ramp. Her collarbone and arm are still broken. Other times people have asked if she wants coffee and then thrown it on her.

How do they survive? "By the grace of God," Marco says. "Every time Cherese goes out with the sign, we pray."

Violence is always a problem. Every time Cherese has been alone she's been robbed or attacked. Once someone tried to break into their RV and when Marco came outside they attacked him with a sledgehammer.

They struggle to keep gas in the RV and have enough food. The cramped quarters also cause conflict and disagreements. But still the RV is better than a tent.

"You gotta do what you gotta do to survive," Cherese says. "You can have so much and lose it all by the snap of a finger."

Three Wishes

1. Get kids back.
2. Clean up.
3. Get a job.

http://invisiblepeople.tv/blog/2009/02/marco-and-cherese/

Hero by Example

by Nedra Weinreich

Mark Horvath is my hero. Not just because he selflessly devotes himself to raising awareness about homelessness, something that most people prefer not to contemplate, but because of how he is doing it. Mark does not just make noise, screaming "Someone has to do something about this problem!" He grabs a bag of socks and heads out to tell the stories of homeless people, one by one. And he pulls the rest of us along at the same time.

The InvisiblePeople.tv project is truly a poster child for what can be done in the social media era. When people complain to me that their budget is too small to make a difference, I point them to what Mark has been able to accomplish with a budget of—essentially—zero. Though I'm sure he would prefer to have a fancy video production and editing set-up, the constraints of his equipment have actually worked in favor of what he is trying to accomplish. The raw, unedited footage parallels the raw emotions that the stories often evoke in viewers.

By giving homeless people a voice, Mark is helping the people most affected by the problem be part of the solution. When he gives them the opportunity to tell their stories, he reminds us that they are human beings first, above all. We can no longer pretend that the shabby figure with the shopping cart does not experience the same emotions we do or that they prefer to live on the street. And Mark has opened our eyes to the fact that beautiful children and babies are homeless, too.

If all the project did was just make us "see" the homeless people we pass every day—that would be a major accomplishment. But the larger picture is that Mark sets an example that inspires others to take action. Mark is one of the biggest mensches that I know. The Yiddish word 'mensch' doesn't just mean a good person, but someone who does the right thing no matter how inconvenient or difficult. Despite the fact that he is constantly on the verge of becoming homeless himself, as soon as he finds out that someone needs assistance, he does whatever he must to help that person.

The biggest payoff of the InvisiblePeople.tv project is that it pushes us to get out of our comfort zone and follow Mark's example.

People are hurting everywhere, so much so that the problem seems overwhelming. But he shows us that each of us—one person at a time, just like Mark—can use our unique talents to help one person at a time.

Nedra Weinreich is a social marketing consultant in Los Angeles who works with nonprofits and government agencies to bring about health and social change. She met Mark on Twitter and has not looked at homeless people the same way since.

Web: www.social-marketing.com/blog/
Twitter: @Nedra

Yong

Greensboro, N.C.

Three months ago Yong lost her house and all of her possessions in a fire. She didn't receive the insurance money she needed and ended up homeless. Before that she was hoping to retire soon.

"I hope one day I can get out of the woods," she says while sitting in her neatly kept and cleaned campsite. She is a survivor.

"The first day I was terrified," Yong says. "I've never been in the woods my entire life. I was afraid of wild animals or people I've never met." At night she stays awake because she doesn't know what's going to happen. Another woman nearby was beaten and raped.

"I talk to God night and day and I get a little bit stronger," Yong says.

Three wishes:

1. People wouldn't forget about God.
2. All homeless people could get a home.
3. Get a home herself.

http://invisiblepeople.tv/blog/2009/09/yong-homeless-greensboro/

Ending Homelessness Requires Social Investors

By David Henderson

You have heard the stories on InvisiblePeople.tv and listened to your heart. You are someone who believes it is wrong that an estimated 3.5 million people experience homelessness across the country every year. While you are right to let your morality lead you to the conclusion that we have to do something about homelessness, you now must let your intellect guide you in crafting an approach to ending it. Homelessness is too serious an issue, and too intricate a social problem, for us to support social programs that fail to deliver measurable social outcomes. If we are to end homelessness, we have to be more than just donors. We have to become social investors.

Homelessness is not just a moral issue; it is a complex socio-economic problem that requires technical sophistication as well as compassion to address adequately. The agencies we support cannot simply provide solutions that sound intuitive; they have to demonstrate measurable progress. In social services, we make a distinction between *outputs*, what an organization does, and *outcomes*, what changes occur in an individual's life as a result of an organization's efforts. For example, an agency might provide a shelter program that houses families for up to 90 days, providing supported services like employment training and counseling. These tactics are outputs; they are the instruments by which an organization tries to reduce homelessness. The outcomes are what happen to the clients at the end of the 90 days. Do people transition to steady employment and housing, or do they remain homeless at the conclusion of the program? Answers to these questions are the outcomes, the changes, if any, which occur in peoples' lives.

As social investors, we must be vigilant in investing in organizations that have measures in place to evaluate their progress and adjust service offerings based on outcomes. When you research organizations to invest in, ask for copies of annual reports. Organizations that focus on enumerating program outputs rather than evaluating social outcomes are likely to be riskier investments than agencies that have a technical eye toward evaluating the progress of their clients. Ultimately, what matters is the impact a social program has on reducing homelessness. If we are to invest in organizations that have the greatest impact, we cannot be distracted

Open Our Eyes: Seeing the Invisible People of Homelessness 73 by focusing on antiquated donor metrics like ratio of program to administrative costs. The bottom line of any homeless services organization is reducing incidences of homelessness, period.

InvisiblePeople.tv not only educates us about the realities of homelessness, it also challenges us to "get mad enough to do something." The message of InvisiblePeople.tv is clear. The end of homelessness begins with us. It begins with us caring enough about homelessness to not wantonly throw money at the problem. Giving money away is easy. Investing is hard. But if we are to really end homelessness, we have to become more than donors, we have to become social investors dedicated to investing in high impact social programs.

David Henderson is the CEO of Idealistics Inc., a social enterprise that builds web-based technologies that help social service agencies help people better. David is a regular blogger on inforumusa.org, fullcontactphilanthropy.com and homelessness.change.org. His thoughts on the social sector have been featured in the *Chronicle of Philanthropy*.

Web: Idealistics.org
Twitter: @David_Henderson

Butch

Cleveland

Butch, now confined to a wheelchair, has been homeless since the summer of 1969. As a teenager his family fell apart and he ended up on the streets. He's been there ever since.

"I'm just out here doing the best I can," Butch says. "I'm living life as a homeless man, but I ain't mad at nobody."

Three wishes:

1. Home with his wife.
2. Be rich.
3. Be super rich.

http://invisiblepeople.tv/blog/2009/11/butch-homeless-cleveland-ohio/

Robert

Los Angeles

Robert and his wife moved to Los Angeles from Las Vegas in search of a better life and housing. They didn't find it and ended up in the city's notorious Skid Row. The problems grew worse when they couldn't find a shelter that would let them stay together.

"I finally had to break down and get a tent," Robert said. "They need to help people who come down here as a family and not split them up."

Robert and his wife have been together for 11 years. Today was his wife's birthday, but instead of celebrating they were spending the day in line for services at a homeless drop-in center.

The one bright point in Skid Row is that you don't have to worry about food. Robert says you can get something to eat 24 hours a day, whether you want it or not.

Three Wishes:

1. To get everybody a house.
2. To give everybody happiness.
3. That the Lord would take care of everybody.

http://invisiblepeople.tv/blog/2009/06/robert-homeless-skidrow/

Social Media Matters

by Wendy Cohen

Mark Horvath and InvisiblePeople.tv exemplify the unparalleled power of social media: Using online tools to organize offline action. Through an innovative video blog and compelling Twitter feed, InvisiblePeople.tv tells the stories of those who are otherwise ignored, and in doing so compel us to acknowledge America's homeless crisis.

In 2009, I began researching homeless organizations to feature in a blog series about ending homelessness as part of the digital campaign for *The Soloist*. It seemed that no report, statistic or traditional news item was able to effectively inspire someone to take action on this seemingly insurmountable issue. Then I discovered InvisiblePeople.tv and it completely altered the way I think about social media. We started cross-posting Mark's videos on the TakePart blog and linking to the often-unsettling stories he tells on his site. Very little seems as vital or effectual as the InvisiblePeople.tv videos that put a face on homelessness; few seemed to tell such a powerful story in 140 characters or less. You simply can't ignore a first-hand account of what it is like to live on the street.

Mark is using technology to document and track a crisis in real time. While there is a value in long-term research and reporting, there is little time to waste with a crisis of this magnitude. InvisiblePeople.tv is able to get to the heart of the problem and solve the most basic and immediate needs, almost instantly. Mark sent out a call for raincoats on Twitter; readers reacted by helping him purchase them in bulk. Mark sent out a call for someone in Seattle to help a friend who had moved there for a job opportunity only to be mugged; within minutes one of Mark's followers on Twitter had approached the man and gave him enough money to get out of the 27 degree weather for the night. This is not only redefining fundraising and drastically cutting down response time, but is also finding solutions that social services are not equipped to provide. There is no doubt that we need national and local organizations working to end homelessness, but for those falling through the cracks, InvisiblePeople.tv has found a way to help.

Social media offers powerful tools to find and mobilize communities around issues. This isn't new. But powerful storytelling is what can turn a video blog and a Twitter feed into a movement and InvisiblePeople.tv is now setting the bar. Mark is changing the face of homelessness and in doing so, has inspired and challenged many to make other crises visible to our communities.

Wendy Cohen is the manager of community and alliances at Participant Media. Before moving to Los Angeles, she was the community manager at the Huffington Post and programmer of the fifth and sixth annual Media That Matters Film Festivals. Wendy co-founded Screening Liberally and produced her first film in 2008.

Web: TakePart.com
Twitter: @TakePart

Donald

New York

Donald is homeless on the streets of New York City. He doesn't have a hard time finding food or even a place to sleep. He struggles to get proper identification so he can claim his Social Security benefits.

"They are attacking the symptoms, not the problem," Donald says, complaining about the lack of help for his specific problem.

Donald has been arrested several times for sleeping outside at various places in the city, including a church.

Through all of this he survives thanks to his strong will, the upbringing he received from his grandmother, his military training and his belief in God.

"When I get my social security my future will be fine," Donald says. "I'll look up my son and I'll pay a visit to my ex-wife. I'll stabilize myself and go on with the next part of my life. I believe that God has something else for me to do. Otherwise I'd be like my friends—I'd be six feet under."

Three Wishes

1. See his son.
2. Stay healthy.
3. Get Social Security.

http://invisiblepeople.tv/blog/2009/10/donald-homeless-new-york-city/

Misconception #6: Band Aids

Whatever I do to help homeless people is just a band aid on a much larger problem and therefore it's not worth doing anything.

This one is also tricky. Because in some ways, it's true. The $1 you give to a panhandler isn't going to get them off the streets. Even offering a bus pass or taking a homeless person out to lunch isn't much. It's a nice gesture, but in the scheme of things it doesn't amount to much.

But imagine it from the perspective of a homeless person. Imagine you've given up on the system and you've lost hope. That single $1 may mean the difference between sleeping outside in the rain and getting into a shelter for the night. That bus pass could mean the difference between walking across town and being able to take a needed nap while you ride the bus.

These are small gestures, but they mean something. More than anything, they mean you were seen, you were noticed, someone cared about you. In many ways it's a matter of perspective—these small acts of compassion can add up and someday might be enough to turn the tide.

At the very least, would you rather everybody ignored you and acted like you were invisible, or would you prefer small, band aid gestures? Even if a band aid doesn't change anything, it at least confirms you're still a human being.

Viper

Los Angeles

Viper is 37 years old, needs a wheelchair, has a catheter and relies on a seizure alert dog named Molly. Last night she slept in the doorway of a Hispanic church on Hollywood Boulevard. While she slept someone stole her walker.

"It's hard for me to do a lot of things," Viper says, "But I do it."

She's been homeless much of her life, thanks to disabilities, foster care and domestic violence. Her health issues and service animal prevent her from being admitted to most homeless shelters.

"I try with all the stress I've been under," she says. "It's not easy."

Despite all of that, she has a smile and a warm sense of humor. She survives by the grace of God, the minimal disability income she gets and the kindness of those who help.

"There's not much help here," she says. "We've no place to go because they kick you out of everywhere you go. It's very hard. You don't know how you're going to be able to eat, do your laundry, get your next chance to clean up again."

She's hoping to get a van to live in and save up enough money to eventually get a place to stay.

Three Wishes:

1. Housing
2. See her 18-year-old daughter before she dies.
3. Just be around her family.

http://invisiblepeople.tv/blog/2009/01/viper/
http://invisiblepeople.tv/blog/2009/07/viper-homeless-hollywood/

I Know Her Story

by Jessica Gottlieb

I've seen homeless people my entire life. I've cooked meals in soup kitchens and celebrated Thanksgiving with the nonprofit Children of the Night. I've been as aware as a suburban woman can be. But I'm guilty of not seeing faces. My intense discomfort with the homeless has made me one of the people who sees them as invisible.

In the autumn of 2009, I had a friend come into town from the Midwest. We went to Hollywood and Highland for supper, and then a walk on Hollywood Boulevard afterwards. As we were walking down Hollywood Boulevard I saw a woman in a wheelchair with a black and white dog. I grabbed my friend Melissa and said, "My G-d Melissa, I know her. I know her story. She's very ill." And chills ran down my spine.

You see, I'd seen Viper profiled on InvisiblePeople.tv just a few days before. I knew that she was ill, that being homeless in a wheelchair was unimaginable. Mark Hovarth's seemingly simple video project made me look at a woman who I would have otherwise walked past.

Everything about looking at homeless people is uncomfortable. It's our societal failure that people just like you and I are marginalized. When I was young my father would remind me that homeless people had mothers and fathers who loved them and kissed them when they were babies.

Last fall I gave Viper some money. She wasn't just a lady with a sign to me. I don't know that the money helped her all that much, but I know I saw her as a fellow human in need.

Jessica Gottlieb is a mommy blogger who lives in Los Angles and is frequently awestruck by Mark Hovarth's incredible actions.

Web: JessicaGottlieb.com
Twitter: @JessicaGottlieb

Cotton

Greensboro, N.C.

Cotton is homeless, disabled and living in a homemade tent in the woods of North Carolina. She's been homeless for 16 years straight. You might think a person could adapt to those conditions after 16 years, but Cotton rejects that idea.

"It's hard every day and there's no end in sight," Cotton says. "Every day takes a piece out of me."

She survives by the 'grace of God,' and is thankful for the food stamps and cigarettes people bring her. But you can also see her anger as she rails against the social services system.

"They can spend hundreds of thousands of millions of dollars to flush it down the toilet but there's not a dime to help us," Cotton says. She can't endure the stress of living in a shelter and that's why she's out here in the woods. "It's brutal, it's cruel, it's senseless—it's so unnecessary."

"What's my future?" She laughs. "My future is throwing myself in front of these freight trains when I can't take it anymore. 16 years is a long time. Talking about a future in these circumstances is ridiculous."

Three Wishes:

1. "World peace," she says mockingly.
2. Cold beer.
3. Cigarettes.

http://invisiblepeople.tv/blog/2009/09/cotton-homeless-disabled-greensboro/

Appreciative

by Stefanie Michaels

I distinctly remember Renee from Operation Smile telling me about InvisiblePeople.tv one morning in a meeting. She told me how the Twitter community was reaching out and embracing this amazing individual, "@hardlynormal." I didn't know his name at the time, but knew I had to get on board and support the far-reaching and brave endeavor of this once homeless man.

The video of a homeless woman and her dog on the streets of Hollywood hit me, too sick to be helped by community services, and with a dog, not allowed in a homeless shelter. I dug deeper and saw a couple who lost jobs, then their home, hoping that their strife would be temporary, though candid about the fear of what was to come, and the idea of "just going home."

Home. Where we hang our hats, where we love, where we cook dinner, bathe, socialize.

InvisiblePeople.tv. Powerful. Perspective. Creating appreciation for what we have. Focus.

It wasn't until months later that this virtual @hardlynormal and I met, and I could finally put a face and name to that voice who interviewed his subjects on the videos so compassionately, the one who tells their stories. Mark.

Mark Horvath. Inspiration. Thank you, Mark, for giving us these amazing people's stories, for giving them a voice and for the opportunity to know you.

You've changed our lives.

Appreciative.

Whether she is swimming with sharks, island hopping in Croatia, spa-ing in Iceland or in zero gravity with Buzz Aldrin, Stefanie Michaels is the go-to-girl for "living life's adventures." She's shared advice for *The New York Times*, CNN, Fox News and *People* magazine. She's one of Twitter's Top Global 100.

Web: AdventureGirl.com
Twitter: @AdventureGirl

Kathy

Austin, Texas

"Miserable," says Kathy, describing life on the streets. "You deal with judgment from others on a daily basis. You deal with the police constantly harassing you. Right now I have over $1,500 worth of tickets in the municipal court."

Kathy describes harassment by the police in Austin and how she's been ticketed multiple times for soliciting.

She has a hard time getting a job because she doesn't have a permanent address. She says employers won't return her calls when she puts a homeless shelter as her address. Last night she slept on a bus bench in downtown Austin.

"I know my future isn't looking very positive here in Texas," she says. Kathy and her husband are considering a move to Florida to find construction work.

Three Wishes:

1. Her kids to come home.
2. A job.
3. A normal life.

http://invisiblepeople.tv/blog/2009/08/kathy/

The Ecological Crisis Impacts Homelessness

by Geoff Livingston

The invisible face of the homeless comes from many places, from job losses and economic hardship to mental issues and alcohol/drug addiction. But there's a new cause emerging: Climate change.

According to the International Organization for Migration (IOM), 20 million people were made homeless last year as a result of sudden-onset environmental disasters. From more frequent and stronger hurricanes to rising sea levels, even the most secure people are threatened. In the next 40 years, this number could rise to a total of one billion people.

Just today an astounding 3.1 percent of the world (again the IOM) is in a migratory state. The extent of homelessness just shocks me.

How can we continue to justify our excessive use of resources, from food and materials to energy and fuel while turning a blind eye to homelessness? Furthermore, this consumption—which causes climate change—is actually worsening the problem. The interconnectedness of our societal problems amazes me.

Mark Horvath talks about the invisible faces of the homeless, the people we consciously pass on the streets without helping. We don't want the difficulty of trying to change their plight. It would simply be easier to tune them out, mindlessly engaged in our iPhones or daily difficulties. That's a shame because they are real people.

I've had various brushes with homelessness in my life. When I lost a job in the dot com bubble in 1999, I ended up moving back to D.C. with the shirt on my back and the computer in the trunk. I lived in a friend's basement for two months until I found a job. I was lucky the situation didn't devolve causing me to live on the street, but it was through the grace of friends and family that I made it. Believe me, I was afraid for the worst.

More recently, I've had the great fortune of doing some work and fundraising for D.C. Central Kitchen. The Kitchen does a wonderful job providing training and opportunities for the city's homeless. Working for a day with these people you see how wonderful they are, their smiles and their newfound lives. It reminds me that no matter what there is still hope.

I've also cooked for the homeless at Miriam's Kitchen. And that, my friends, was so sad. It was early in the morning, and you can feel the anger and the hurt of the homeless as they waited outside for their food. Pain penetrated the air.

Writing this as I wait out yet another major snowstorm—an unprecedented third major storm for one winter (hello, climate change)—I have to wonder how the city's citizens, the ones who are forced to live on the street will do. And then there are those who may become homeless because of this ongoing winter crisis. Isn't it time to stop and really pay attention to this problem?

Geoff Livingston co-founded Zoetica, a social enterprise that provides superior communication consulting, training and strategy to help mindful organizations affect change. Some of his professional experiences include United Way of America, Save Darfur, Environmental Defense Fund, Live Earth, ChildFund International, the Philanthropy 2.0 Project and many others.

Web: ZoeticaMedia.com
Twitter: @GeoffLiving

Steve

Los Angeles

"Homeless is tough," says Steve, "but I am tougher." Steve is a self-described romantic. He came to Hollywood to sell his screenplay, "The Late Bloomer," which he keeps securely in the bottom of his shopping cart.

"At 6 a.m. I start pushing a cart in search of aluminum cans, plastic bottles and glass and hope to make enough money for beer and cigarettes," Steve says. "I eat food entirely out of dumpsters." Steve is 58 and has been homeless for nearly four years since he lost his job in Las Vegas.

"I have $8 in my pocket right now, so I feel rich," Steve says. "I'm from the Hamptons, by the way." He spends his nights in an alley.

"No matter how bad things are on the outside—and they are bad for me right now—I still love being alive," says Steve.

http://invisiblepeople.tv/blog/2009/05/steve_homeless_hollywood/

Misconception #7: Let the Pros Do It

Helping the homeless is for the professionals. Let them do it.

This is another tricky misconception because in many ways it is true. The professional social service agencies are truly the ones helping the homeless right now. They can likely mobilize volunteers and donations far more efficiently than you can. They know how to respond, they know the resources available and they know what to do.

But it's not all about efficiency. Nobody wants to be marched through a social service agency like cattle. The professionals may know what to do and how to do it, but you can still show kindness. You don't have to be a professional to do that.

Helping the homeless isn't a job we can just outsource to someone else. If homelessness is ever going to be truly addressed, then the non-experts need to care. The non-experts need to stand up and do their part. It's pretty hard to screw up love.

In the end this enormous job isn't just for the professionals. In many ways the professionals need your help. They're outmanned and outgunned. They can't do it all and there are so many ways you can help.

Don't let the professionals be an excuse to keep you from getting involved.

Open Our Eyes: Seeing the Invisible People of Homelessness

Karen

Detroit

Karen is waiting for a Section 8 housing inspection before she can move into her new residence. She's living on the streets while she waits. So far it's been three weeks of waiting.

Last night she slept on a cot on the sidewalk. She's frustrated living among drug users and dealers who "hate on each other."

When asked how she survives, Karen shrugs and says, "The best way I can."

Three wishes:

1. Money.
2. Peace of mind.
3. Housing.

http://invisiblepeople.tv/blog/2009/12/karen-homeless-detroit/

Invisible People: Hardly Heard... Hardly Seen... Hardly Normal

by Lee Fox

Coins jingling in a cup, a cardboard sign held up,
A hungry mouth that pleads,
It's hardly heard.

Quickened paces in our walk, looking down so not to talk,
Someone's sleeping in the streets,
It's hardly seen.

No place of their own, fallen and alone
People struggling with great need
It's hardly normal.

Mark Horvath strikes a nerve—and this is perhaps his most effective tool. Though oft described as an advocate for the homeless, I see Mark more as an agent of change.

When I first heard Mark talk about his cause—and refer to the homeless as "invisible people," I felt a flush of shame. Despite my own philanthropic practices, more often than not, I had been in the habit of averting my eyes from their uncomfortable reality.

It's like a punch in the gut when you realize that there are 35.9 million people (and 14 million children) in the United States living in poverty—many at imminent risk of becoming "invisible" should they take to the streets.

As someone who works in the cause and social impact space (specific to online and real-world engagement) I see Mark as an extraordinary case study in the best practices of social media for social good.

Mark is a mastermind in that he is capable of humanizing each member of this outcast society—one person at a time. By crisscrossing the United States and capturing their stories with video, photos and micro-blogs, Mark gives a new face to homelessness. One tale after the next, Mark's success is measured by how much harder he makes it for any one of us to turn a blind eye.

Those who have built a relationship with Mark through the foundation of social media might marvel (as do I) at the choice selection of his online name. Juxtaposed against "Invisible People," Mark's Twitter handle, "Hardly Normal," serves to punctuate the unhealthy relationship that exists between "them" (the homeless) and "us" (society).

It is 'hardly normal' that so many of our own face such dire circumstances. And though I am not entirely sure he would agree, I see Mark more driven by a need to educate the rest of us on how to become better advocates for our nation's poor siblings, parents and children, than to save those less fortunate than himself.

On the other hand, Mark is "hardly normal," having been invisible himself for a few years before reclaiming his own identity as a functioning member (whatever that means) of our society.

Mark, thank you for opening my eyes.

Lee Fox is the founder of KooDooZ—a cause-based youth empowerment website. Working with profit-for-purpose and nonprofit organizations to create signature cause-campaign "challenges," Lee pairs youth passion with action for social change. When turning these challenges into achievements, participating youth can earn community and/or service learning credits, in addition to making a difference.

Web: KooDooZ.com
Twitter: @KooDooZ

Tracy

Austin, Texas

"I want to get out of here," Tracy says. She lives in a weekly rate motel with her husband and four kids. It costs $250 per week—$1,000 per month—which is about what an apartment would cost in Austin. But they have a hard time paying first and last month's rent and the deposit up front. Plus a lower credit rating can disqualify families.

"This is not what I really wanted," she says. "Sometimes you have to take whatever you can get." Their motel is an upgrade from the last one. Before they only had one room, now they have two bedrooms, a living room and a kitchen.

Tracy's husband works full-time but she can't find a job.

"I want my kids out of this environment," she says.

Three Wishes:

1. Get a good job.
2. Get a house or an apartment.
3. A better environment for her kids.

http://invisiblepeople.tv/blog/2009/08/tracy-homeless-families-austin-texas/

When is Enough Enough?

by Chloe Noble

I sit here wondering how I am going to explain to you what is going on. There is no longer any time left for quaint and moving stories that urge our fellow neighbors to hand out a few bucks or spend a holiday at one of our local food kitchens. What is happening on the streets of America begs us to answer the questions Martin Luther King Jr. placed before us years ago: "Where do we go from here? We are called upon to help the discouraged beggars in life's market place. But one day we must come to see that an edifice which produces beggars needs restructuring. It means that questions must be raised."

As I stand among the millions of homeless—some layered four generations deep now—in this land of plenty, in this free world of great opportunity, I am appalled at how we can allow children as young as 12 years old to roam the streets alone at night not knowing where their next meal is going to come from. That is just the tip of the iceberg. The unspeakable things I have witnessed and experienced living with these homeless youth have broken my heart and have pierced my spirit in a way that can never heal. Not until every homeless child is seen and heard, not until every homeless individual is treated with the dignity and respect that *each one* of them deserves.

Will we continue to allow ourselves to be fragmented and continuously segregated as a nation, or will we rise up empowered and truly free, and become *the people* we are meant to be? I believe we can. I believe we will.

Mark Horvath, and others like him, are paving the way to a world where all people are treated equally, no matter how difficult their situation is. What message is it sending when we not only ignore the homeless epidemic, but at times actually kick them while they're down? InvisiblePeople.tv is an organization that stands not only to ensure that the homeless in America are finally seen and heard, but that they are also empowered and inspired to become who they are meant to become.

The homeless are a microcosm of what we as a nation are suffering from, trying to heal from and trying to rise above. As long as we continue to fragment ourselves by class and live in the isolation of complacency, we will not grow to see what phenomenal and beautiful things we are truly capable of. The only way we can evolve effectively out of the social degeneration that exists in this country is to reach out our hands and grasp one another in a genuine embrace of determination and complete faith in something bigger than ourselves. If others could only see the homeless from their advocate's perspective, their hearts would be filled with so much unexplainable beauty that they would never be the same again. Both the suffering and the beauty run deep. And we are going to show this country that they are no longer allowed to be blind to either.

God bless you, Mark Horvath. May your "invisible people" one day rise from the underground and unseen nation they are, into the limelight and surround us everyday.

Chloe Noble is the founder of PrideWalk2009 where she and Jill Hardman completed a 6,000-mile journey to raise awareness of the homeless youth epidemic. She is also the founder of Operation Shine America, a nonprofit organization for homeless youth that inspires and empowers the public through personal, local and national activism.

Web: OperationShineAmerica.org
Twitter: @ChloeNoble

James

Detroit

James went from making $90,000 a year to living on the streets. He worked in the auto industry, took an early buyout and went back to school. When he graduated he couldn't find any opportunities and quickly ran out of money. Then he lost his house.

With what little money he had he turned to boarding houses. "They're really bad," James says. "Worst places in the world." When he completely ran out of money they kicked him out in the street.

James spent four weeks living on the street, begging for food and sleeping in abandoned buildings. He eventually entered a program where a collection of some 80 local churches would provide meals, bus passes and a place to sleep.

But it's still far from easy. "You're sick all the time," James says. "You're on an 800 calorie diet. I lost 30 pounds in 30 days."

Most recently he entered a program that went beyond the basics. They gave James a haircut and helped him open a checking account so he could access his retirement funds. Now he'll be receiving Social Security checks and can make it on his own.

Three wishes:

1. "Nothing else. Got everything I need."

http://invisiblepeople.tv/blog/2009/12/james-homeless-detroit/

God Loves Invisible People

by Scott Williams

I remember driving to church this one particular Saturday afternoon as though it were yesterday. I came upon an intersection that was commonly infused with homeless people and panhandlers. I will generally hand over a few dollars or just smile to the regulars, but that day I noticed a new and unfamiliar face.

As my car came to a complete stop waiting for the light to turn green, this new kid on the block began to stroll down the lane of cars. He was a middle-aged black man with a solid blue T-shirt, some dingy jeans, black shoes and a hat that was pulled down low so I could just see his eyes. He held up his sign and it read "Homeless Please Help."

I gave this gentleman a few dollars and told him God loves him and he simply responded, "God bless you sir, you don't know how much that means."

Over the next few months I got to know Kevin. I would periodically drop off some food from Wendy's and watched Kevin as he got on his feet and found work. He even managed to show up at my church a time or two.

Over the months Kevin disappeared and literally became invisible. Each morning I passed through the intersection I would wonder what happened to Kevin and why he disappeared. One morning I proceeded to the stoplight of a totally different intersection in a totally different part of town. This intersection had quickly become the high traffic hotspot for homeless people and panhandlers.

As I approached the stoplight of the intersection there was a middle-aged black guy who looked like Kevin—no wait, it was Kevin. I quickly pulled into the parking lot across the street so I could go holler at my long, lost invisible friend Kevin. As I walked across the street, I could see Kevin smiling from ear to ear and we embraced with a hug.

Kevin said words to me that I'll never forget; he said and I paraphrase, "Scott, it's good seeing you. I just want to say thank you for looking at me as a person and realizing that we are not all out here trying to get a drink or do drugs. I appreciate every meal that you have ever given me, every kind word that you ever shared with me, every dollar that you ever gave me and most importantly taking the time out to say, 'Kevin I love you and God does too.' It's easy to lie down under a bridge and think that people have forgotten about you and no one really cares. Thanks for caring!"

Although it's easy for us to pretend that we don't see the invisible people with the cardboard signs, it's important to understand that many of these invisible people don't need money. They need someone to care. If we remember that, "Then the King will say, 'I'm telling the solemn truth: Whenever you did one of these things to someone overlooked or ignored, that was me—you did it to me.'" (Matthew 25:40, *The Message*).

God loves "invisible people."

Scott is a pastor at LifeChurch.tv. Prior to ministry Scott served in various leadership roles as an entrepreneur, lobbyist, professor and strategist. At the age of 25, Scott was one of the youngest prison wardens in the country. He is an author, avid blogger and social media enthusiast.

Web: BigIsTheNewSmall.com
Twitter: @ScottWilliams

Jay

Cleveland

Jay's story is devastatingly familiar today. He lost his job to the economic downturn and then his house to foreclosure.

"It's extremely difficult these days," Jay says. He's been homeless for two years now.

He has found organizations and services that provide help, but he's frustrated by the bureaucratic system that sends him chasing aid from different providers.

"It's like you get the run around everywhere you go," Jay says. "You spend your time spinning your wheels not getting what you need." He'd like to see consolidated services to make it easier to get the help people need.

Jay survives with a little bit of help from food stamps, a few friends, shelters, churches that provide meals and faith.

Three wishes:

1. "That everyone would treat everyone as equals. The man that has a $100,000 job is no better person than the guy that's picking up garbage on the corner. We're all the same, we're all human beings. Why can't we just help each other?" Then Jay added, "And I think if everyone did that I might not even need two more wishes."

http://invisiblepeople.tv/blog/2009/11/jay-homeless-cleveland-ohio/

5 Practical Ways You Can Help the Homeless

Reading a book like this can be hard. Thanks for having the guts to read it and not simply ignore it. But now it's time to do something about what you've just read.

Below are five practical ways you can help the homeless. It's not a complete list and there are many other ways you can help. The important thing is to do something.

1. See the Homeless as People
Mark Horvath named his site InvisiblePeople.tv because of the way so many homeless people feel invisible. People ignore the homeless, they look the other way, they pretend not to see a fellow human suffering.

Perhaps the greatest thing we can do to help the homeless is to actually see them. We need to see the homeless in our midst and recognize that they are people not so different from ourselves. We need to treat them with the respect and compassion that every human deserves.

A kind, supportive word and a smile can go long away.

2. Stand Up for the Homeless
Not only are the homeless invisible, but they're often voiceless. They often cannot defend themselves, both in a theoretical and tangible ways. The homeless don't have lobbying organizations or lawyers to protect their civil rights. They're also vulnerable to all kinds of violence, from unkind words to physical attacks.

You can be the voice that stands for homeless people. Educate yourself about the plight of homelessness. Then stand up to support them. Speak out against legislation that would be harmful or support new laws that would be helpful. Educate others about the reality of homelessness and dispel the myths. Take a strong stand against violence and ensure that the homeless are not being denied justice.

3. Give

Donate cash to support organizations that help homeless people. There are so many shelters and programs that help and they rely on your financial support.

Give supplies to organizations that help or hand them out yourself to homeless individuals. This can be any kind of basic need, including food, clothing, personal hygiene items (toothbrush and toothpaste, antiperspirant, comb/brush, tampons, etc.), hats and gloves, blankets, sleeping bags, tents, diapers, etc. Remember that not all homeless people will need all of these items—don't assume that just because they're homeless they need whatever you have to give. Ask what they specifically need and provide that. A family shelter may need toys or books or pillows. Find a need and come up with a creative way to meet that need.

4. Volunteer

You can volunteer your time and your skills to help homeless people.

Volunteer your time: Team up with organizations that already help the homeless and find out how you can help. This can range from staffing a shelter to serving soup to entertaining kids while their parents fill out paperwork.

Volunteer your skills: No matter what your skill you can help the homeless. You can teach on the job skills like carpentry or clerical work. You can offer services like counseling, medical care or legal advice. You can help homeless people apply for jobs, government aid or navigate the dizzying array of social service options. In some cases a car and a phone is the only thing keeping a homeless person from getting the help they need.

5. Come up with a Plan to Help

Depending on where you live you'll interact with homeless people in different ways. In an urban area you might see them in the park near where you work. In a suburban setting you might see them at exit ramps where it's difficult to engage in conversation. You might find that the homeless are even less visible in your area, pushed away in encampments in the woods or living quietly in shelters.

Wherever the homeless are in your area, find a way to help them in your specific situation:

- You could stock the glove box of your car with gift certificates and granola bars for the panhandling homeless at exit ramps.
- You could print up a list of local organizations that serve the homeless in your area and have it ready to hand out.
- You could buy a bag of socks and spend your Saturday morning passing them out and hearing each individual's story.
- You could commit to volunteering once a week at the local shelter.
- You could connect with a homeless person and help them with job applications, securing a P.O. Box or whatever it is they need help with.

Whatever it is you can do, come up with a plan and put it into action.

Remember to always look out for your own safety and avoid confrontation.

A Word from Mark

Hi, this is Mark. Yup, that Mark Horvath you've been reading about. I know Kevin didn't want me to write anything for this book only because he knows how slammed I am and he didn't want to burden me. But after just reading it I had to say something. I am beyond wrecked!

I am honored that anyone would take the time to do this, and to write good things about me and the homeless cause. I am still blown away that I inspire anybody to do anything except lock their doors as I walk by.

As much as I've tried to hide my own story, I know I am part of the homeless story. When I started InvisiblePeople.tv I wanted to anti-brand it. I wanted you to notice John, Jennifer, Popcorn and Tracy's kids—not the marketing—and especially not me. But the more I tried to hide my story, the more you all started to talk about me.

That said, there is another story here. There is a story about how anyone with the desire to effect change can make a positive impact on our world. I would probably bet that you have something in your heart that you'd like to do. Well, if I can effect real change so can you. The hardest part is facing your own fear. The fear that it won't work, or people won't accept it, or it's too hard, or you don't have the resources, and all the other road blocks we give ourselves to keep us from moving forward. Here's the secret—take action and move forward. The rest will work itself out.

I am honored that some people call me a hero. I don't consider myself as such. In fact, I'm really not that nice. I'm just a hardly normal guy trying to navigate through an abnormal world by helping others. If I look at the world today and all the madness I want to crawl in a hole and pretend all is fine. It's not! But if I take simple, tangible actions to make our world a little better my world gets a little better along the way.

As our world gets worse we must get better!

I'm grateful for all the people who took the time to write a little something, and I am so very thankful to all of you who bought this book to support InvisiblePeople.tv. You are all my heroes. But the people I need to thank most are the hundreds of homeless people who had the courage to allow us into their lives. Becky Kanis once said to me, "anonymity is death." So often we try to bury painful topics, but without the real truth being told there will be no change.

InvisiblePeople.tv is not just a website with videos; it is a conversation about real change. My hope is that something here has changed you enough to keep the conversation going.

Many hugs and much love,

Mark Horvath
InvisiblePeople.tv
Chief Evangelistic Officer, Do-Gooder and Loud Mouth

Acknowledgements

Thank you:

To you the reader for buying this book and supporting InvisiblePeople.tv.

To the crew who helped create this book: Brian White, Michael Buckingham, Ronald Cox, Bradley Watson, Josh Cody and the untold number who will help spread the word.

To the contributors: Brad Abare, Chris Brogan, Wendy Cohen, Lee Fox, Jessica Gottlieb, Alan Graham, David Henderson, Jeff Holden, Michael Ian, Becky Kanis, Natalie Profant Komuro, Jeff Lilley, Geoff Livingston, Heather Meeker, Brandon Mendelson, Stefanie Michaels, Scott Monty, Shannon Moriarty, Chloe Noble, Stephanie Rudat, Kari Saratovsky, Lisa Truong, Nedra Weinreich and Scott Williams.

And of course, Mark Horvath.

Made in the USA
Lexington, KY
15 November 2010